AF674299

The Exemplar Beyond Compare

Muhammad Mustafa

صلى الله عليه وسلم

Osman Nûri TOPBAŞ

ERKAM WORLD
INTERNATIONAL ISLAMIC PUBLICATION

© Erkam Publications - Istanbul: 2023 / 1444 H

The Exemplar Beyond Compare

Muhammad Mustafa

ﷺ

Osman Nuri Topbaş

Original Title: Emsalsiz Örnek Şahsiyet
Author: Osman Nuri Topbaş
Translator: Erdinç Atasever
Copy Editor: Süleyman Derin
Publisher: Abdullah Şenyiğit
Graphics: Rasim Şakiroğlu
ISBN: 978-81-19946-34-1
Address: İkitelli Organize Sanayi Bölgesi Mahallesi
Atatürk Bulvarı, Haseyad 1. Kısım No:60/3-C
Başakşehir, İstanbul, Turkey
Tel: (+90-212) 671-0700 pbx
Fax: (+90-212) 671-0748
E-mail: info@erkamworld.com
Web site : www.erkamworld.com
Language: English

ERKAM WORLD
INTERNATIONAL ISLAMIC PUBLICATION

بسم الله الرحمن الرحيم

İstanbul - 2023 / 1444 H

Allah, glory unto Him, presents the Noble Messenger ﷺ in the following manner:

"And We have not sent you but as a mercy to the worlds…"

(al-Anbiya, 107)

"O Prophet! Truly We have sent you as a witness, a bearer of glad tidings, and warner; and as one who invites to Allah's grace by His leave, and as a lamp spreading light."

(al-Ahzab, 45-46)

"Certainly you have in the Messenger of Allah a quintessential example for him who hopes in Allah and the Latter Day and remembers Allah much."

(al-Ahzab, 21)

بسم الله الرحمن الرحيم

İstanbul - 2023 / 1444 H

Allah, glory unto Him, presents the Noble Messenger ﷺ in the following manner:

"And We have not sent you but as a mercy to the worlds…"

(al-Anbiya, 107)

"O Prophet! Truly We have sent you as a witness, a bearer of glad tidings, and warner; and as one who invites to Allah's grace by His leave, and as a lamp spreading light."

(al-Ahzab, 45-46)

"Certainly you have in the Messenger of Allah a quintessential example for him who hopes in Allah and the Latter Day and remembers Allah much."

(al-Ahzab, 21)

"Nay, verily for you is a Reward unfailing; and you stand on an exalted standard of character."

(al-Qalam, 3-4)

"O Believers! Obey Allah and obey the Messenger, and render not your actions vain."

(Muhammad, 33)

"Whoso obeys Allah and the Messenger, they are with those unto whom Allah has shown favor, of the prophets, the saints, the martyrs and the righteous. The best of company are they!"

(an-Nisa, 69)

"Allah and His angels send blessings on the Prophet: O Believers! Send your blessings on him and salute him with all respect."

(al-Ahzab, 56)

Foreword

Eternal praise and appreciation to our Glorious Lord for granting us the honor of being among the *ummah* of Muhammad Mustafa ﷺ, hailed as the Beloved of Allah and thus the crown of all prophets.

Eternal greetings to our Blessed Prophet ﷺ, the Undying Sun, whose unique character has shed an unfading light of guidance and truth on entire mankind endeavoring on the path of perpetual bliss.

Mankind was perplexed in its darkest hour that Allah, glory unto Him, sent him as a prophet, offering him thus as a present, a relieving mercy to the world, just when it was grappling at the throes of oppression and gloom. Raised by Allah from the distant horizon, the Prophet ﷺ was like a glittering star shining above a world densely clouded by the ignorance of a society more brutal, heedless and disruptive than beasts.

Simpler put;

Allah, glory unto Him, granted the Prophet ﷺ as an eternal mercy for beings living and lifeless alike, from dust and stones, to rivers and seas, a blessing for the earth as well as the skies, for both space and time; but in particular for human beings, as their unfailing means for attaining salvation, guidance and mercy.

Such a mercy the Prophet ﷺ is, that beings were created only in his honor and valued in Divine Sight only in accordance with the love they nurtured for him.

Such a mercy he is, that sheltered underneath the wings of his compassion is not only entire humankind but also the whole realm of being.

Such a mercy he is that he has been presented by the Glorious Lord as an everlasting source of grace endowed with incomparable attributes, an abundant fount of life for all parched hearts.

Such a mercy he is that through him was tendered the Sacred Quran, the book of perpetual guidance.

Such a mercy the Blessed Prophet ﷺ is that he stands as the most beloved of Allah, the Merciful and the Compassionate, and as the one graced with the exclusive gift of *Miraj*, the Ascension.

Such a mercy he is that without him, the entire universe would have turned into a harsh desert.

Such a mercy he is, that creation was launched through his Light.

Such a mercy he is that the beautiful is always his reflection, created solely for his sake. Nowhere does a flower bloom that is not of his Light, for had it not been for him, nothing would have been. He is for whose sake we are. He is an unfading blossom of sheer light cultivated by the Divine that only blooms fresher by the day.

Such a mercy the Prophet ﷺ is that it is the Almighty Himself who explains his worth; by sending His greetings too.

Under the roof of prophethood of that Exceptional Mercy did the entire universe receive a taste of true peace. Suffocated till then from the smoke of its rebellion, humankind was able to set sail to higher ground, through the door of wisdom unlocked by the Blessed Prophet ﷺ, and inhale a new breath of life. Consciences of stone melted in his graceful hands. Hearts polluted by dirt and rust were cleansed to purification in his crystal fount, becoming pure abodes of love.

Prior to receiving guidance, the Abyssinian Wahshi, for one, was an atrocious savage, a brute who feasted on blood. But by virtue of submitting to the Prophet's ﷺ sublime training, he ended up becoming a teary eyed Companion. Many alike, before their guidance, were spiritually dead, fatally wounded by the claws of vice. Yet, later drinking from the very same spring of guidance enabled them to become forever young, to achieve a respect that will eternally accompany their names.

Confirmed by all this is the fact that, both inwardly and outwardly, the Blessed Prophet ﷺ is the greatest sample of art ever fashioned by Allah, glory unto Him. The noblest, he is moreover the most perfect and beloved, such that the great figures of wisdom and courage that have appeared on the scene of earth throughout history are only reflections of the Prophet of Grace ﷺ, portions of that magnificent exemplar, moonlights mirroring that luminous Sun who has been presented as a gift of mercy, by Allah, to every single realm of existence.

The road that leads to Allah, glory unto Him, and his pleasure therefore naturally passes through a love of and abiding by the Beloved Prophet ﷺ, a fact illustrated by the Almighty in the *ayah* of the Quran below:

قُلْ اِنْ كُنْتُمْ تُحِبُّونَ اللّٰهَ فَاتَّبِعُونِى يُحْبِبْكُمُ اللّٰهُ
وَيَغْفِرْ لَكُمْ ذُنُوبَكُمْ وَاللّٰهُ غَفُورٌ رَحِيمٌ

"Say, if you love Allah then follow me so that Allah will love you and forgive your faults; and Allah is Forgiving, Merciful." (Ali Imran, 31)

مَنْ يُطِعِ الرَّسُولَ فَقَدْ اَطَاعَ اللّٰهَ وَمَنْ تَوَلّٰى
فَمَآ اَرْسَلْنَاكَ عَلَيْهِمْ حَفِيظًا

"Whoever obeys the Messenger indeed obeys Allah, and as for whoever turns back…We have not sent you as a keeper over them." (an-Nisa, 80)

Thus expressed is the reality to which nobody, who believes in the Almighty, can remain insensitive and indifferent. As emphasized by the Quran, the sole measure of loving Allah is adhering to His Messenger ﷺ, like a moth around a flame. *Iman*, that is belief in Allah, glory unto Him and the entirety of what He has revealed, cannot otherwise be in the truest sense of the word. It ought to be known that no other path remains in endearing oneself to Allah, glory unto Him; and without endearing oneself to Allah, all deeds are in vain.

The Blessed Prophet ﷺ must therefore always be located in the center of our lives and in the core of our hearts, and his

unrivalled, exemplary character allowed to be the architect in fashioning ours.

And doubtless to accomplish that, we need to get to know him more intimately and gain a greater acquaintance, until we breathe his breath and our hearts beat as one, just like the Companions, the devoted lovers of the Prophet ﷺ.

Being the lackluster souls we are, even though nurturing an intense love of the kind the Prophet ﷺ no doubt deserves may lie beyond our reach, just being on the road thereto should be considered an enormous bliss in itself. Besides, receiving just a share of the reflection of his exquisite character will suffice to open the gate of eternal happiness.

It is thus only to gain a closer acquaintance with the Prophet's ﷺ noble character that we have attempted to write the work at hand, albeit with an ink of inadequacy and weakness. It is a concise summary of what has been mentioned in our previous works with regard to the sublime disposition of our Blessed Prophet ﷺ.

Our words are certainly not worthy of him, though be that as it may, we are all compelled express gratitude for the greatest Divine gift through explaining his ways and embodying them in our lives. To the best of our ability, it remains our single most supreme duty to act as bridges conveying his endless mercy and peace that encompasses the whole extent of being to our contemporary phase of history engrossed in and battling crises of peculiar kinds. It is our debt of loyalty to communicate such zenith of Divine Art to the rest of mankind, as much as our speech permits. But without a shadow of a doubt, the most supreme honor lies in representing him in the best possible manner through adopting his conduct.

May the Glorious Allah grant each of us shares of the exemplary character of the Prophet ﷺ and turn our hearts into palaces of love… May he endow us with success in the grueling test of piety in adhering and submitting to the Noble Messenger ﷺ and hence bless us with Divine love and pleasure!

Amin…[1]

1. I pray Allah, glory unto Him, to turn the efforts of our precious students, who have helped bring this work to fruition, into *sadaqat'ul-jariyah*, a reward never ceasing.

Part One

- The Exemplar Beyond Compare
- Uswat'ul Hasana / The Quintessential Example

The Exemplar beyond Compare Prophet Muhammad Mustafa ﷺ

The pages of the book of prophetic history were first turned with the presentation of the Light of Muhammad to the first man, coming to a close with the bodily manifestation of Muhammad ﷺ on Earth. Simpler stated, from the first moment, this exalted Light proceeded through the purest and noblest genealogical lines until reaching Abdullah, from whose forehead it then passed onto Aminah, the fortunate mother pregnant with the Light of Being, wherefrom it was eventually handed over to its true owner, the Prophet ﷺ, the Most Excellent of creation.

The fascinating system that is the universe, owes its existence to the Light of Muhammad ﷺ. Flows of Divine Power perceivable throughout the universe and numerous patterns of beauty to be seen in full view are simply reminders, glimpses of that Light. As alluded to in the below excerpt from a hadith, the only reason the heartfelt repentance of Adam عليه السلام was accepted was because the dust from which he was created had a grain of the dust of the Prophet ﷺ:

"'Lord…I ask Your forgiveness for the sake of Muhammad!' pleaded Adam عليه السلام after realizing his error for committing the blunder that led to his expulsion from Paradise.

Then Allah, glory unto Him, asked:

'How do you know Muhammad when I have not yet created him?'

'When You created me,' said Adam عليه السلام *'and breathed into me from Your Spirit, I looked up and saw the words* ***La ilaha ill'Allah Muhammadun Rasulullah*** *inscribed above the pillars of the Throne. I knew there and then that You would only mention the most beloved of all creation next to Your Name.'*

Thereupon Allah, glory unto Him, declared:

'You have spoken the truth, Adam! Surely, he is the most beloved for Me of all creation! So implore me for his sake; and since you have, I hereby forgive you. ***Had Muhammad not been, you would not have been created!'"***[2]

Submitting the name of Muhammad ﷺ as a means, a *wasilah* in his repentance, Adam عليه السلام was able to receive Divine Amnesty. The Muhammedan Light then proceeded forth, becoming temporarily embodied in Ibrahim عليه السلام, whereby the fire of Nimrod was tamed to coolness and pleasance; and as a pearl enclosed in the wrapping that was of Ismail عليه السلام, it induced the sending of a ram as sacrifice from the Heavens.

As can be seen, even prophets made the most of Divine Mercy through his name. There were even those like Musa عليه السلام who yearned to become simply a number among his *ummah*, just to reap the blessings of his adherence, as illustrated in a hadith narrated by Qatadah ibn Numan رضي الله عنه:

"*Musa* عليه السلام *once prayed:*

2. Hakim, *al-Mustadrak ala's-Sahîhayn,* Beirut 1990, II, 672/4228.

'My Lord…On the Tablets[3] *You have given me, I see there is mentioned a virtuous nation brought forth from among mankind, enjoining good and forbidding evil. Let them, oh Lord, be my nation!'*

'They are Ahmad's nation!' *replied Allah, glory unto Him.*

'Lord…I see made mention in the Tablets a nation last to appear on Earth yet poised to enter Paradise first. Let them be mine!' then pleaded Musa ﷺ*.*

'They are Ahmad's', *the Almighty responded once more.*

'The Tablets mention a nation who recite their Scriptures by heart, from memory, whereas those before needed their written Scriptures in front of them to read and would not remember a letter of it once their Scriptures had vanished. You have without a doubt given this nation, my Lord, a power to memorize and protect, of a kind You have not given any nation before. So let them be mine!'

'They are Ahmad's', *declared the Almighty once again.*

'My Lord,' continued Musa ﷺ*. 'Mentioned there is a nation, who believe both what has been revealed to them and before them, who persevere against all kinds of deviance and the one-eyed impostor Dajjal. Please, let them be mine!'*

'But they are Ahmad's', *stated Allah, glory unto Him.*

'The Tablets refer to a nation, my Lord, who are given a reward just for intending to do a good deed, even if they do not carry through with it, and if they do, are rewarded ten to seven hundred times in return. I beg to You to make them mine!'

3. Pages of the Torah.

'They are Ahmad's nation', *Allah declared.*

Thereupon Musa ﷺ *put the Tablets he had been holding aside, and pleaded:*

'Then my Lord, make me member of Ahmad's nation!'"[4]

Thus each ring of the chain of prophets, each a flame of guidance in their own right, were auspicious harbingers of the coming of Muhammad Mustafa ﷺ, sent as mercy to the entire realm of being.

And At long last, in the year 571, on the Monday morning of the 12th of Rabiulawwal, the anxiously anticipated Light arrived at the world of manifestation to honor the entire extent of space and time, from the bountiful marriage of Abdullah and Aminah,

Divine Compassion overflowed throughout the universe with his arrival. Days and nights changed complexion. Feelings grew deeper, tastes profounder; everything gained a unique meaning, a peculiar elegance. Idols collapsed, crumbling to pieces. The grand pillars and towers of the pretentious palaces of Medain, the domain of Persian Emperors, fell apart. Akin to the swamp of ignorance that was to suffer the same fate, the Lake of Sawa dried up. Hearts became filled with a grace and prosperity that encompassed the entire universe and the whole spatiotemporal scope alike.

Had the Blessed Prophet ﷺ, the epitome of all virtues, not made his honorable arrival to the world, mankind would have been left struggling in the throes of oppression and brutality

4. Tabarî, *Jâmiu'l-bayân an tawîli âyi'l-Qur'ân,* Beirut 1995, IX, 87-88; Ibn Kathîr, *Tafsîru'l-Qur'âni'l-Azîm,* I-IV, Beirut 1988, II, 259, (in the commentary of A'râf, 154).

until the end of time, leaving the weak captive at the hands of the strong. The pendulum would have swung in the favor of evil, at the expense of balance. Earth would have been a haven for oppressors and tyrants, a sentiment elegantly reverberated in the poem:

Messenger, had you not have come,
Roses would not have bloomed,
Nightingales would not have sung,
To Adam, the names would have forever remained unknown
And left without meaning,
Being would have been left to mourn...

Mawlana Rumi ﷺ, that great voice of Truth, propounds the degree of gratitude we ought to feel for the Noble Prophet ﷺ, who for a life time endured the most unthinkable of hardships to shatter the idols and overthrow oppression:

"*You, who today enjoys being a Muslim; know that had it not been for the supreme effort of our one and only Ahmad ﷺ, and his resolve in smashing the idols, you too would have been an idolater like your forefathers.*"

Not only did the wisdom and knowledge laden content of what the 'Unlettered Man', who appeared in an ignorant society remote from civilization, leave the people of the time in awe, it also bequeathed to posterity a miraculous ocean unfathomed and indeed unfathomable till the Final Hour. Attesting to this is the fact that even though the Sacred Quran touches upon a variety of issues from the recounting of past events to the foreboding what is to come of social and scientific nature alike, for what is now over 1,400 years, no discovery has been able to disprove its assertions. Yet even the most prestigious encyclopedias today are afflicted with the recurring need of self-correction and improvement by way of publishing additional volumes and appendixes each year.

That orphan and unlettered Prophet ﷺ never received any education from any one person; still, he proved to be a savior of entire mankind, a translator of the realm of the unknown and a master of the school of Truth.

Musa عليه السلام had conveyed certain laws. Dawud عليه السلام excelled through the prayers and psalms inspired in him by Allah, glory unto Him. Isa عليه السلام was sent as an exemplar of virtue and piety. Muhammad Mustafa ﷺ came with all of these. Pronouncing laws, he at the same time taught ways of refining the self and praying to Allah with a pure heart. The paramount virtues he taught, he epitomized throughout his life. He advised not be beguiled by the deceiving dazzle of the world. Succinctly said, he embodied all the rights and duties of the entirety of prophets before him. The nobility of both lineage and conduct, of beauty and perfection were personified in him.

Forty years among an ignorant society, he spent, during which most of the perfections he later was to promote remained a mystery to nearly all of them. He was not known as yet as a man of state. Little were aware of his orating abilities. Speaking of his potential as an illustrious commander was one thing; he was not renowned even as an ordinary soldier.

Still without a doubt, the fortieth year of his life proved to be the most extraordinary turning point in the course of the history of humankind.

Before that, nobody had heard him talk about the histories of peoples and prophets of the yesteryears, or of paradise and hell. Reputed only for leading a distinctive life of utmost virtue and solitude, that momentous return from the Cave of Hira where he was entrusted with Divine duty, marked an incredible change.

Once he began the invitation, entire Arabia was left in shock and awe, enthralled by the eloquence of his call. Contests of poetry and literature the Arabs had reveled in until then suddenly became devoid of essence. Nobody no longer dared to hang their prize winning poetry on the wall of Kabah, laying to rest an age old tradition; such that the sister of the famous poet Imr'ul-Qays, reputed for her depth of poetic insight, upon hearing the Quranic verse:

وَقِيلَ يَآ اَرْضُ ابْلَعِي مَآءَكِ وَيَا سَمَآءُ اَقْلِعِي
وَغِيضَ الْمَآءُ وَقُضِيَ الْاَمْرُ وَاسْتَوَتْ عَلَى الْجُودِيِّ
وَقِيلَ بُعْدًا لِلْقَوْمِ الظَّالِمِينَ

"Then the word went forth: O earth! Swallow up your water, and O sky! Withhold (your rain)!" and the water abated, and the matter was ended. The Ark rested on Mount Judi, and the word went forth: Away with those who do wrong!" (Hud, 44), remarked:

"This leaves us all lost for words. Even my brother's poems can boast no more", immediately after which she brought down the *qasidah* of Imr'ul-Qays pinned on the uppermost part of Kabah's wall, leaving no other choice for the other lesser poems of the *Muallaqat*, fastened below it, than to be taken down.[5]

5. Ahmed Cevdet Paşa, *Kısas-ı Enbiyâ ve Tevârih-i Hulefâ,* Istanbul 1976, I, 83.

The Messenger of Allah taught ﷺ entire mankind, in the flesh, the truth of his being the Prophet of the Real, glory unto Him. He instated only the most perfect principles pertaining to society, culture, economy, governance and international relations, the inner wisdoms of which would take even the most preeminent scholars and scientists a lifelong experience of research, into both man and matter, to grasp. To be sure, humankind will better appreciate the Muhammedan Truth, as it further develops in theoretical knowledge and practical experience.

The remarkable Prophet, who had never before laid his hands on a sword, without previous military training except for participation in only one battle, and that as virtually a spectator, unfolded to be a courageous soldier, a competent commander in way of the struggle of *tawhid* and the enforcement of social peace, in spite of exuding a compassion vast enough to encompass the whole of mankind.

He communicated the religion of Allah, glory unto Him, from door to door notwithstanding the preferences of the hapless to shut their doors insolently on the face of the Sun of Guidance and forever remain in their crass darkness. Their hearts of stone at times provoked them to treat him rudely; yet the Prophet ﷺ never took their rudeness personally, only grieving on behalf of them, for their careless ignorance.

To such people, he always simply stated:

"No reward do I ask of you for this (Qur'an), nor am I a pretender." (Sad, 86), reminding them he had but the pleasure of Allah in mind.

In a matter of nine short years, he triumphed over the entire Arabian Peninsula, almost always with forces a third the size of the enemy; and what's more, with minimal loss of lives on both sides. Instilling a spiritual power and a military training to the hitherto unruly group of people granted him a miraculous success in the said campaigns, such that those to follow after him would end up routing the two strongest and most dominant powers of the time, in Byzantine and Persia.

Realizing the greatest revolution in the history of humankind, in spite of the inauspicious circumstances, the Prophet of Allah ﷺ thus effaced the oppressors, wiping the long shed tears from the eyes of the oppressed. His sacred hands became combs for the heads of orphans. Hearts were freed from grief with his comforting touch.

Enunciating this beautifully is Mehmed Akif:

Then the Orphan had matured and reached forty,
Bloody feet stomping on heads, till then, were flushed,

With a breath, the Innocent saved all mankind,
A strike, and the Caesars and Khosraus were brushed,

Revived were the weak, the sole right of who was to suffer,
And oppression, no one would think it would, was crushed,

A Mercy to the Worlds, indeed, was his Clear Way,
And he got, whosoever wanted justice as their hide,

Whatever the World has, it is all but His offering,
To Him is obliged society, and so the individual obliged,

Obliged is all of humankind to that one Innocent, oh Lord
Revive us in the Hereafter with this thought on our mind!

The prophethood of Muhammad Mustafa ﷺ is akin to a boundless ocean, with those of the remaining prophets analogous to rivers pouring into it. A cut above all the previous prophets, reportedly around 124,000 in number, in all their eminent traits known and unknown alike, he has come to represent the zenith of perfection in virtuosity. Setting a standard for humanity in his time, in all aspects of their hitherto developed thought and ways of life, he in addition is a quintessential point of reference for what needs may arise until the Day of Judgment; for which reason he is *the* Prophet of the Final Hour.

In confession of being endowed with supreme morals, the Blessed Prophet ﷺ is in fact known to have said:

"*I have been sent to complement good morals.*" (Muwatta', Husn'ul-Khuluq)

Having left behind him no worldly property worth the scantiest of value, the Prophet ﷺ nonetheless bequeathed the most precious legacy conceivable, a towering morals and character.

Uswat'ul-Hasanah / The Quintessential Example

Muhammad Mustafa ﷺ is the only prophet, and in fact, the only man in history to have every intricate detail of his life recorded. Only a limited account of the flawless conducts of other prophets, inherent with the resources of providing guidance for mankind and steering to what is good, have survived till today. But with an inner world of feeling thoroughly monitored, moment by moment, as it became actual in the simplest to the most involved of his words and actions, the ways of the Prophet of the Final Hour ﷺ have been thoroughly preserved as befits the most precious heritage in history, awarded through the grace of Allah with the furthermore privilege of an assurance of survival till the very last man to come until the Final Hour.

Resisting failure at the face of the various trials and tribulations life has to offer compels us to place trust in the Almighty, be at peace with destiny, uphold patience, courage and perseverance, be altruistic and generous, with a contentedness and a richness of heart, and hold a steady balance against the possible discrepancies of the given circumstance. The *murshid'ul-kamil* par excellence in exercising all these virtues as typified through a pure and exemplary life is Muhammad Mustafa ﷺ, the most generous gift of Allah, glory unto him, to humankind.

The life of the Blessed Prophet ﷺ provides a splendid example for all generations to come until the Last Day. Of him, the Quran states:

"Nay, verily for you is a Reward unfailing; and you stand on an exalted standard of character." (al-Qalam, 3-4)

The life and the gracious character of the Prophet ﷺ mark the apex of human conduct, even simply with his pattern of behavior that is graspable by human understanding. The pinnacle of prophets and the archetype of human character who completed his mission in the midst of society by setting the best of examples to emulate, the Almighty has presented him to mankind as, in the words of the Quran, *uswat'ul-hasana*, the quintessential example.

Thus states the Holy Quran:

لَقَدْ كَانَ لَكُمْ فِى رَسُولِ اللّٰهِ اُسْوَةٌ حَسَنَةٌ لِمَنْ كَانَ
يَرْجُوا اللّٰهَ وَالْيَوْمَ الْاٰخِرَ وَذَكَرَ اللّٰهَ كَثِيرًا

"You have indeed in the Messenger of Allah a quintessential example for any one whose hope is in Allah and the Final Day, and who engages much in the Praise of Allah." (al-Ahzab, 21)

In all stages of life, the Noble Prophet ﷺ offers a brilliant perfection for all eyes to see, exuding all kinds of beautiful conduct, whether in concise or in detail. Whatever the most perfect forms of conduct there may be to follow, one may therefore find its epitome in the sublime life and the Sunnah of the Prophet ﷺ.

Muhammad Mustafa ﷺ is *the* religious leader and *the* head of state. He is an example for those entering the garden of Divine Love, and no less for his gratitude and humbleness when abounding in the blessings of Allah.

Just as he is an example for his patience and trust in Allah, glory unto Him, in times dire, the Prophet ﷺ is also an example for his generosity with and personal abstinence from the spoils of war. He is an example for extending the abundant compassion he had for his family to the slaves, the weak and stray; and all the more in his magnanimity and lenience towards the guilty.

Thus If you are wealthy, then ponder on the ***humbleness*** *and* ***generosity*** *of that Great Prophet who reigned sovereign over entire Arabia and won over the hearts of every Arab notable through love...*

If you are among the weak, then take reference from the Prophet's ***life*** *in Mecca under the rule of the horribly oppressive idolaters...*

If you are triumphant, reflect on the Prophet of ***courage*** *and* ***submission*** *who routed the enemy at the battles of Badr and Hunayn...*

But, Allah forbid, should you become defeated, then remember the Prophet walking ***patiently*** *and* ***courageously*** *amid his wounded and martyred Companions at the field of Uhud, having completely yielded to Divine Will...*

And if you are a teacher, just think of the ***delicate, sensitive*** *and* ***affectionate*** *Prophet conveying the pearls of his heart to the Students of Suffa by the Masjid'un-Nabawi ...*

If you are a student, picture the Prophet sitting before Jibril ﷵ *at the moment of Revelation,* **cautious** *and* **motivated***, filled with* **respect***.*

If you are a preacher, a counselor calling to the good, then give ear to the pleasant voice of the Prophet flashing sparks of **wisdom** *from his heart to his Companions at the Masjid...*

If you are left without an aid in your want to protect and communicate the Truth and elevate it, then take a look at the life of the Prophet who **proclaimed the Truth** *to the ignorant and called them onto guidance at a time when he was deprived of all aid in Mecca...*

If you have broken the resistance of the enemy, leaving them incapacitated, and devastated evil to proclaim the Truth, then bring before your eyes the sight of the Prophet, on the day of the Conquest, humbly and **thankfully** *entering the sacred turf of Mecca, on camelback as if to fall prostrate, despite being a victorious commander...*

If you own a farm and want to put things on track, then draw a lesson from the Prophet of **competence** *who appointed the most able to* **revive** *and* **administer***, in the best possible way, the lands of Banu Nadir, Khaybar and Fadak after seizing possession of them...*

If you are lonely, then reflect on the son of Abdullah and Aminah, their dearly loved **orphan of innocence***...*

If you are a teenager, closely consider the life of the youth, the future prophet, shepherding the stock of Abu Talib at Mecca...

If you are a trader set out with caravan loads of goods, ponder the integrity of the grandest man of the convoys destined for Yemen and Damascus...

If you are a judge, recall his ***just*** *and* ***prudential*** *move in intervening to replace the Black Stone at the verge of Meccan notables going at each others' throats…*

Then turn your glance once more to history and take a look at the Prophet in Medina at the Masjid'un-Nabawi delivering his verdict with ***the greatest conceivable justice*** *between the poverty stricken destitute and well to do rich, as just as one can imagine.*

If you are a spouse consider the ***deep emotions*** *and* ***compassion*** *of the Blessed Husband of Khadijah and Aisha…*

If you are have children then learn the affectionate conduct of the father of Fatimah, the grandfather of Hasan and Husayn…

Whoever you may be and in whichever circumstance you may find yourself in, you will find Muhammad Mustafa ﷺ as ***the most perfect master*** *and* ***most beautiful guide*** *at all times and places.*

Such a master he is that one can correct all mistakes through emulating his Sunnah; and putting things back on course, make amends for all misplaced efforts. Following the light of his guidance, one will at once rid his path of drawbacks and find himself reach the gates of happiness…

The inner world of the Blessed Prophet ﷺ, to be sure, is an exhibition far more exquisite than a garden of paradise bursting with rare and elegant flowers and charmingly scented roses.

Truly evident is hence the fact that the life of the Prophet ﷺ constitutes the most perfect example, even for those on opposite poles of the social plane. The life of a convict, for instance, can never provide an example for a judge, just as a judge cannot be shown as an example to a convict. Likewise, the fate of one grappling with poverty and struggling to earn a living throughout her life can never provide a case in point for one wealthy abounding in riches. But the life of the Blessed Prophet ﷺ affords an example for both ends of the scale, for the reason that making him begin his journey of life from the lowest social end as an orphan, the Almighty proceeded him through each arduous stage of life till finally elevating him to the apex of power and authority, as prophet and head of state.

Each phase the Prophet ﷺ underwent throughout the course of his life abundantly exhibits ideal modes of behavior to abide by in accommodating the ebbs and tides of human life in general. Thus in whatever position and circumstance one may be encumbered by, compliant with their means and capabilities, the life of the Noble Messenger ﷺ offers concrete and perfect examples of actions to adopt and implement for all people.

He is thus the grandest masterpiece transpired by Allah, glory unto Him, in mankind. The exemplar par excellence for society to emulate, from the lowest end of the scale to the highest, for Believers steeped in his inimitable character, the Prophet of the Almighty ﷺ is, at once, the ideal criterion in practice.

Apart from prophets and the righteous who follow in their wake, everyone with the pretense of showing humankind the road to salvation, with the false air of being a guide for the rest to follow, and in particular philosophers attempting to explain everything with their limited rational capabilities and cognition, are eternally doomed to betray deficiency. Since they are firmly grounded in Divine Revelation, all prophets have come as guides of Truth confirming one another. Each have communicated and instructed the commands sent by Allah, always quoting the Almighty, conveying His commands.

Yet it has always been their personal views that philosophers, posing as guides in shedding upon mankind the light of Truth, have expounded, insofar as they have been deprived of Divine reinforcement in their words and have thus had to infer under the influence of their egos, tainted by their inadequate reasoning. All they have accomplished therefore is refuting and disclaiming the systems of one another, falling miserably short of guiding themselves let alone the rest of society.

Aristotle, for instance, though known for having founded certain principles of ethics, being devoid of Divine Revelation, seeing a single person affirm faith in his system and find happiness through its application is inconceivable. True to form, the hearts of philosophers have not been refined; neither have their souls been purified and their thoughts and actions matured through the unique aid of Revelation.

The only means of protection from the abysses that rational faculties and inner inclinations untrained by Revelation may steer one towards, is the *Habl'ul-Matin*, the Toughest Rope presented to humanity by the Prophet of the Final Hour ﷺ, which is the Holy Quran. And the most tangible and practical realizations of the truths found deep in the bosom of the Quran are to be observed in the prosperous life of the Blessed Prophet ﷺ. Standing as the most urgent task for man compelled to fulfill his reason for existence is therefore to align in accordance with the Quran and Sunnah.

For the Quran and the Sunnah are the prescriptions of happiness for both Here and the Hereafter, the eternal legacy of the Light of Being ﷺ who has bequeathed those two luminous beacons for his *ummah.*

Before embarking on the duty of prophethood, the Blessed Prophet ﷺ had moreover endeared himself to everyone, by virtue of a perfection exuding character that simply compelled all to confess to him being *the* Trustworthy *–al-Amin-* and *the* Honest *–as-Sadiq-*. Only subsequent to this affirmation of character did the Call begin.

Fully aware of the Prophet's ﷺ exemplary character of decency and integrity long before the arrival of the great duty, the locals cherished him. The Tribe that called him *al-Amin* had equally succumbed unconditionally to his adjudication amidst an embittered dispute regarding the replacement of the Black Stone during the renovation of Kabah. For the Messenger of Allah ﷺ was pervaded with such honesty that even Abu Sufyan, still an infidel nurturing only malice for the Prophet ﷺ at the time, when posed a question by Heraclius, the Byzantine Emperor, regarding whether there was ever a time that the Prophet ﷺ did not keep his word, had no other option than to answer, unswervingly:

"Never…Every promise he makes, he keeps." (Bukhari, Bad'ul-Wahy 6, Salat 1, Sadaqat 28; Muslim, Jihad 74)

A further testimony to the extent the pre-Islamic Arabs trusted Noble Messenger ﷺ are the words of Abu Jahl, the archenemy of the Prophet, and his friends:

"By God, Muhammad, we do not dispute you…for our part you are an honest and decent man. We only dispute that which you have brought!"

Revealed in relation was the below *ayah*:

"We know indeed the grief which their words do cause you. It is not you they reject but the signs of Allah, which the wicked contemn." (al-Anam, 33)[6]

Even his most bitter enemies had recognized the noble Muhammad ﷺ as a true prophet in their hearts, rejecting him nonetheless because of their deluded egos.

Another incident shedding light on as to why the Light of Being ﷺ was dubbed *al-Amin* even by his foes runs as follows:

The Battle of Khaybar continuing, a shepherd from Jewish ranks by the name of Yasar came to the Prophet ﷺ and after a brief conversation expressed his desire to enter the fold of Islam. Hospitable, the Blessed Prophet ﷺ nevertheless required him first to return the sheep to their owners;[7] and this at a time when the battle had already overstretched the time limit and a shortage of supplies had begun to emerge as an immediate crisis among Muslim ranks...The consideration doubtless provides a glaring exhibition of the importance of responsibility, awareness of duty and safekeeping what one has been entrusted with, even during the most difficult times.

As for deriving the utmost benefit from the excellent conduct and virtue of the Noble Prophet ﷺ, it is consequent upon

6. Wâhidî, *Asbâb'u Nuzûli'l-Qur'ân,* prepared for publication by Kemâl Besyûnî Zağlûl, Beirut 1990, p. 219.
7. Ibn Hishâm, *Sîratü'n-Nabî,* Beirut 1937, Daru'l-Fikr, III, 397-398; Ibn Hajar, *al-İsâba,* Beirut 1328, Dâru Ihyâi't-Türâthi'l-Arabî, I, 38-39.

reaching the level of the submission of Abu Bakr ؓ, exemplified by his remarks on the *Miraj*:

"If he says he has gone there, it must be true!"

Innumerable manifestations of justice, compassion and mercy throughout the life of the Prophet ﷺ stand as exemplary acts to imitate for the entire world till the Final Hour. No unprejudiced eye that has enjoyed the privilege of a moments gaze at the dazzling light radiating forth from that Incomparable Chandelier can dare to dispute his reality, even if it remains concealed within their conscience. Many a foreign scholar, felt obliged to bow to his reality despite remaining a nonbeliever, has given voice to his inner acknowledgement of the virtue and success of the Blessed Prophet ﷺ. One such figure is Thomas Carlyle, who has described his birth as:

"...the slipping out of light from darkness."

Written in the Encyclopedia Britannica, confirmative of the virtue of the Noble Prophet ﷺ, is the following:

"Neither a prophet nor a reformist has verged upon the success of Muhammad in the whole history of humanity."

Similar is the remark of B. Smith:

"Without the least doubt, Muhammad is unanimously the greatest revolutionary."

Writer Stanley Lane-Polo makes a clean breast with the below confession:

"The day Muhammad forged the greatest victory against his enemies was also the day he acquired the greatest victory of virtue in himself; for the day he conquered Mecca, he let

Quraysh go free of blame, rendering it an official amnesty effective for the entire Meccan community."

A comparable disclosure is made by writer Arthur Gilman:

"We witness his grandness during the Conquest of Mecca. The effects of past torments he was inflicted with could have very well actuated in him feelings of revenge. But Muhammad rather prevented his army from shedding even a drop of blood. Showing a majestic compassion, all he did was thank God."

A rigorous research of numerous legal systems well before the proclamation of the Declaration of Human Rights, enthused La Fayette, a philosopher renowned as being one of the masterminds behind the French Revolution of 1789, to appreciatively proclaim the supremacy of Islamic Law:

"Muhammad the Magnificent...! You have attained to such a towering peak of justice that it has been impossible, and so shall it remain, for anyone to surpass it!"[8]

How great a virtue it must be that compels even the enemy to affirm and admit its verity...Such is the virtue and integrity of the Blessed Prophet ﷺ, testified to all along by even the staunchest of disbelievers...

The exceptional life of Muhammad Mustafa ﷺ has embodied a moral perfection more than sufficient to separately light the way, at once, for a variety of activities. He constitutes the focal point of the education of the entire corpus of mankind, throwing sparkles on the way of those seeking the

8. See Kâmil Mîras, *Tecrîd-i Sarîh Tercemesi*, Ankara 1972, IX, 289.

grandest illumination. Offering guidance through unwavering and illuminative light for all in search of the true path, he is the sole master of humanity.

The avid circle of learners flocked around him was virtually a college that had enrolled persons from all levels in society. Regardless of the color of their skin, the disparity of their languages, and despite the copious variety of their cultural backgrounds and seemingly irreconcilable social differences, they would gather there, as one. Nothing stood in the way to hinder anyone wishing to join in the circle. There, was not reserved exclusively to any one tribe; it was rather a font of knowledge and wisdom valuing men and women insofar as they were human beings. And thus obliterated were all differences between the weak and strong…

Just take a look at those to have adhered to the Prophet ﷺ; you will see men of prominence of the likes of the Abyssinian King Najashi, the Ma'anian notable Farwa, the chieftain of Khimyar Dhul'qila, Firuz Daylami, the Yemeni notable Maraqaboud and the governors of Umman Ubayd and Jafar.

Sure to strike you at a second glance, however, over and above the kings and chieftains aforementioned are disfavored men such as Bilal, Yasir, Suhayb, Habbab, Ammar, Abu Fuqayha among others, and vulnerable and unprotected women like Sumayya, Lubayna, Zinnirah, Nahdiya and Umm Abis.

Among the illustrious Companions were people of supreme wit and intelligence endowed with a sense of precise judgment, just as there were those with competence to solve the most intricate of problems, steeped with insight into matters worldly, adept in governing vast lands with proficiency.

The adherents of the Blessed Prophet ﷺ were to end up ruling grand towns and vast regions. It was through their efforts that many were granted access to guidance and a taste of justice. They spread peace and serenity among people, fusing them like brethren.

Part Two

- The Towering Morals of the Prophet of Allah ﷺ
- Standards from the Stars

The Towering Morals of the Prophet of Allah ﷺ

The history of mankind presents no other figure besides Muhammad Mustafa ﷺ, whose every feature of character has inspired so much interest and every intricate detail of life has been scrupulously recorded. Voluminous books could not suffice if an attempt was to be made to explicate each and every feature comprising the overall exemplary character of the Noble Prophet ﷺ.

Fundamentally[9] and *ijtihad*[10] wise, Islamic Sciences have also adopted the various qualities of the Messenger of Allah ﷺ as key proofs, the very reason for the attempts of various disciplines to appraise separately the distinct attributes of the Blessed Prophet ﷺ.

To be sure, all works compiled within the Islamic tradition the past 1400 odd years have been motivated with the

9. The fundamentals upon which Islamic Sciences are predicated are the Quran and Sunnah, collectively referred to as *nass*. Comprising the Sunnah are the Noble Prophet's consenting-disapproving words, actions and behavior. Matters clearly given verdict by the Quran and Sunnah allow no room for *ijtihad*.
10. Ijtihad is the process undertaken by the *mujtahid*, the trained Scholar licensed to pass verdict, to settle a given issue within a specific methodology passed silent by the Quran and Sunnah, again loyal to the bounds of the Two Fundamentals.

ultimate aim of spelling out a book, that is to say the Quran, and a man, the Prophet of Allah ﷺ.

To truly comprehend the Prophet ﷺ, a masterwork of creation, within the restricted bounds of mortal capacity is impossible, insofar as sensory impressions and elucidations thereof are forever inflicted with inadequacy in understanding and explaining him. Just as it is a sheer impossibility to pour an ocean into a cup, so is the comprehension of the Light of Muhammad ﷺ as befits its splendor.

What we will only try to present here, as much as our comprehension allows, will therefore be just a few drops from the grand ocean of the exemplary character of the Messenger of Allah ﷺ, with the anticipation that it will provide service towards gaining an acquaintance with him.

The Prophet of Allah's ﷺ Beauty of Countenance and Morals

The Blessed Prophet ﷺ is a marvel without compare, a beauty of appearance matched by a wonderfully led life. Beyond reach it would be to eloquently describe the Prophet's ﷺ flawless appearance and existence. As stated by Imam Qurtubi:

"The beauty of the appearance of the Messenger of Allah ﷺ did not fully transpire. Were the entirety of his beauties to be shown candidly, with all their reality, the Companions would not have had to power to gaze at him."[11]

11. Ali Yardım, *Peygamberimiz'in Şemâil,* İstanbul, 1998, p. 49.

Indeed, even among those constantly by the side of the Blessed Prophet ﷺ, there were not many Companions who could stare at his beautiful appearance to their hearts content, held back by their sense of *adab*. It has even been narrated that all the Companions would habitually lower their gaze while conversing, apart from Abu Bakr and Omar, supposedly the only two to have ever made eye contact with the Prophet ﷺ; with glowing smiles they would stare at the Noble Messenger ﷺ, who would amiably reciprocate. (Tirmdhi, Manaqib, 16/3668)

This is amply described, in his elderly years, by Amr ibn As ؓ, who made his mark in history as the Conqueror of Egypt:

"*Though I spent a lot of time next to the Messenger of Allah ﷺ, the shyness I was overcome with in his presence and the immense feeling of reverence deep inside always prevented me from lifting my head and staring at his sacred and beautiful face to my heart's pleasure. If they were to ask me, right now, to describe the appearance of the Messenger of Allah, believe me, I could not.*" (Muslim, Iman, 192)[12]

Intimating dependability and trust to those around, the Prophet's ﷺ face was the cleanest and most handsome of all. Upon hearing of his arrival in Medina, the curious Abdullah ibn Salam, then a Jewish scholar, visited the Prophet ﷺ, and after a fleeting look at his countenance, remarked:

"Such a face can never lie", and immediately became a Muslim there and then. (Tirmidhi, Qiyamah, 42/2485; Ahmad, V, 451)

Endowed with an immense degree of beauty, awe inspiring majesty and a dazzling elegance, he really needed neither

12. Also see, **Ahmad** ibn Hanbal, *al-Musnad,* Istanbul 1992, IV, 199.

an extra proof, nor a miracle to prove the truth of him being the Prophet of Allah.

Whenever the Blessed Prophet ﷺ was displeasured, and likewise whenever he was pleased, one could immediately see it in his expression.

His pure body had embodied an intense vigor, a strong sense of *haya* and a rigorous determination. As for the depth of the sensitivity of his heart, it is impossible to articulate.

A lovely light radiated from his face; there was a graceful flow in his speech, elegance in his every move, an extraordinary power of expression, and a supreme eloquence in every word that spilled from his tongue.

Never uttering a word in vain, his every word conveyed wisdom and advice. There was not the least place for backbiting and futile talk in his vocabulary. He would talk to people in accordance with their capacities.

He was kind and humble. Although he would never express his joy through excessive laughing, his face always put a warm smile on view.

Seeing him instantaneously would overwhelm one in awe; though a brief conversation would suffice to implant feelings of deep love and affection towards him.

He would treat the righteous with respect, according to their ranks of piety. Receiving a massive share of his kindness and respect were his relatives. It was habitual for him to extend the tenderness he nurtured for his family and friends to the rest of society.

He would treat his servants inexpressibly well, to the effect of feeding them whatever he had and donning them in whatever he would wear. Generous and compassionate, the Prophet ﷺ had struck a perfect balance between courage and kindness, compliant with the circumstance.

Ineffable is his profundity of benevolence and generosity, even far greater than one who offers without the least fear of destitution.

In the words of Jabir ﷺ:

"He is never known to have said 'No' to anyone who wanted something from him." (Muslim, Fadail, 56)

The most to frequent his relatives, to show the greatest affection and mercy to the public, to treat people in the most beautiful of manners, the most to desist immorality and the most exaltedly virtuous was the Gracious Prophet ﷺ.

"There is nothing heavier on a Muslim's scale of goodness in the Hereafter than good morality. Allah, glory unto Him, despises those with ugly behavior and nasty words," was something he would remind. (Tirmidhi, Birr, 62/2002)

The Messenger of Allah ﷺ was a man of his word, a keeper of his promises. Superior to all in terms of virtue, intelligence and sharpness, his value could not possibly be overstressed.

With that said, he also carried a perpetual look of sorrow. Withdrawn to an uninterrupted state of contemplation, he only spoke when necessary. Though his spell of silence was lengthy, he would complete every sentence he begun, collecting layers of meaning in just a few words; no wonder he was the *Jawami'ul-Kalim*, able to convey the deepest meaning using the least possible words. His words would come out piecemeal, like beads of a rosary. With a gentle predisposition, his stature was nevertheless majestically imposing.

Never would he lose his temper, unless there was an infringement of Divine right; and given there was, his anger would not subside until the right was restored. And afterward, he would once again resign to his usual composure. Getting angry on his own behalf was not his thing; he would never develop a vendetta and become quarrelsome in a personal matter.

He would never enter the household of anyone without permission. Once he returned home, he would divide the time he would spend there into three: the first for Allah, glory unto Him, the second for his family and the third for himself, though only by name, as in effect he would spare that time for all kinds of people, common and elite, depriving not a single person of his precious time, leaving not a single heart unconquered.

At mosques, he would assume different places for seating, to prevent others from making a habit of sitting in a particular place, wary of the consecration of certain places. He disliked the adoption of conceited behavior in public. Upon entering an assembly, he would take whatever seat available, advising others do the same.

Whenever a person wanted something from him in sorting out a particular problem, irrespective of the importance of the favor, the Blessed Prophet ﷺ would never feel at ease until that need was aptly taken care of. Given the impossibility of sorting the problem out, then the Prophet ﷺ would not recoil from at least soothing the person with some comforting and heartening words. He was a confidant for all. No matter what their social classes were, whether rich or poor, wise or ignorant, people would receive even treatment next to him, solely from the vantage of being a human being. All his gatherings were environments teeming with kindness, wisdom, manners, patience and trust, first and foremost in Allah, glory unto Him, then in each other.

Never would there be a person explicitly condemned for his shortcomings. When the need would appear to warn a particular person, the Noble Messenger ﷺ would do as little to subtly yet elegantly hint at it, without breaking the person's heart. Not only was he ever preoccupied with investigating the concealed flaws of others, he was stern in prohibiting others from getting busy with such ignobility.

The Light of Being ﷺ would not speak, unless with an aim to reap Divine pleasure. The assemblies in which he spoke were havens of rapture. The enthusiasm and wholeheartedness that would take over those listening around him when he spoke, was later to be described by the Companions as follows:

"We would sit so quietly and still, as if a bird had perched on our heads and we were afraid that we might scare it to flight." (Abu Dawud, Sunnah, 23-24/4753)

The manners and conduct that had reflected onto his Companions were of such intensity that, more often than not, even asking him questions would be deemed impudent. Thus they would wait for a Bedouin to perhaps arrive from the desert and inadvertently drop in to ask the Prophet ﷺ questions and spark a conversation, from whose blessings and grace they would be in hope of benefiting.

Throughout his life the Blessed Prophet ﷺ was a monument of sincerity. He never said anything which was not already in his heart and never advised anyone to do something he did not. With such inspiring morals, he was the Quran come-to-life.[13]

The Humbleness of the Prophet of Allah ﷺ

Despite achieving, in a very short time, what other kings could have only dreamt of and conquering peoples' hearts as an ideal edifier, the Messenger of Allah ﷺ continued leading his hitherto humble life, taking not the slightest notice of the worldly riches that lay before his feet. Like before, he carried on living modestly in his unassuming **mud** room, sleeping on a mattress stuffed with date leaves. He wore simple clothes. His standard of living was below par even of the poorest of people. At times, though he found nothing to eat, he still remained thankful to Allah, glory unto Him, wrapping a stone around his stomach to ease his hunger. Even though all his sins, committed or impending, had been forgiven, he persevered in his supplication and gratitude to the Almighty, persisting in his lengthy *salats* until daybreak, to the point where his soles would swell. He ran to the aid of the needy. The solace for the orphans and the lonely, by no means did he allow his greatness to get in the way of supporting the underprivileged, taking each and every one of them under his benevolent, caring wings of mercy.

On the day of the Conquest of Mecca, when in the sight of men he appeared the strongest, to a Meccan, trembling in fear and anxiety in the presence of the Prophet ﷺ pleading him to:

13. See, Ibn Sad, *at-Tabaqâtu'l-Kubrâ*, Beirut, Dâru Sâdır, I, 121, 365, 422-425; Haythamî, *Majmau'z-Zawâid*, Beirut 1988, IX, 13.

"Please...Teach me Islam", the Gracious Prophet ﷺ taught him first calmness, with the gentle words reminiscent of the severe bygone years:

"*Calm down my brother, for I am not a king,*" and continued in reference to his honorable late mother, "*...but the orphan of your old neighbor of Quraysh who used to eat sun dried meat*";[14] thereby presenting, what is beyond the shadow of a doubt, the apex of humbleness unprecedented in the entire history of mankind.

Again, on the same day, to Abu Bakr ؓ, the *Yar-i Ghar,*[15] who had carried his aged father on his back to presence of the Prophet ﷺ, requesting him to teach him the words of faith, he benevolently said:

"*Why did you exhaust your elderly father all the way here? Could not have we visited him instead?*"[16]

The Messenger of Allah ﷺ always confessed vulnerability, describing himself, in the words of the Quran:

"I am only a mortal like you; only that I receive Revelation..." (al-Kahf, 110)

Accentuating the clause *abduhu*, i.e being a servant of Allah, in the testimony of faith, he was thus wary, lest his *ummah* fell in the pits of deviancy like others before.

To those who showed excess admiration of him, he would be quick to remind:

---

14. See, Ibn Majah, At'imah, 30; Tabarânî, *al-Mu'jamu'l-Awsat,* II, 64.
15. Yar-i Ghar means the Friend of the Cave, in reference to the companionship of the Light of Being with Abu Bakr in the Cave of Sawr en route to Medina. The term has also been used to describe sincere friendships.
16. See, Ahmad, VI, 349; Haythamî, VI, 174; Ibn Sa'd, V, 451.

"*Do not elevate me above my deserved rank, for Allah made me a servant long before He made me a Messenger.*" (Hayhtami, IX, 21)

The Blessed Prophet ﷺ had a food bowl, called *gharra*, carried by four persons. After having prayed the *duha salat* in the morning, they brought the *gharra* full of stew, around which the Companions then gathered. After there had gathered a many people, the Prophet ﷺ also kneeled down and occupied a little place to give space to others. A Bedouin onlooker, somewhat disillusioned by the behavior he deemed too modest, remarked:

"What kind of a sitting style could that be?"

"*Allah, glory unto Him, created me a dignified and humble servant,*" replied the Light of Being ﷺ, "*not a stubborn tyrant!*" (Abu Dawud, 17/3773)

Thus he declared, in no uncertain terms, that he could never behave with conceit and arrogance.

Again, on an occasion, he professed:

"*No single person can enter Paradise solely through his deeds,*" to the utter astonishment of the Companions who asked:

"Not even you?"

"*Yes,*" the Prophet ﷺ replied. "*Not even me, had it not been for the grace of my Lord. Not even I can enter Paradise unless I am enfolded by His grace, compassion and mercy...otherwise my deeds can not save me!*" (Bukhari, Riqaq, 18; Muslim, Munafiqun, 71-72; Ibn Majah, Zuhd, 20; Darimi, Riqaq, 24)

By pointing to the garb of disgrace awaiting in the Hereafter those who dress out of conceit, arrogance and vanity, the Noble Prophet ﷺ again warns his people against the flames of Hellfire. Some of the hadith in relation include:

"*On the Day of Judgment, Allah will not deign to look in the face those who drag their clothes on the ground out of conceit.*" (Bukhari, Libas, 1, 5)

"*Whoever wears the dress of fame on Earth, Allah shall make them wear the attire of disgrace in the Hereafter.*" (Ibn Majah, Libas, 24)

Without giving it a second thought, the Prophet ﷺ would even donate spoils that fell to his personal lot, preserving a lifestyle of humbleness akin to the materially underprivileged lower class of his *ummah*.

The Generosity of the Prophet of Allah ﷺ

The Prophet ﷺ always referred to himself as a mediator of charity, with a constant emphasis that it is Allah, glory unto Him, who is the Real Giver and Owner of all.

Still not a Muslim, Safwan ibn Umayya, one of the notables of Quraysh, accompanied the Messenger of Allah ﷺ in the campaigns of Hunayn and Taif. Observing the noticeable wonder with which Safwan was gazing at a particular batch of the war spoils gathered at Jiranah, the Noble Messenger ﷺ asked him:

"*Do you really like them?*"

And when Safwan replied in the positive, the Prophet ﷺ said:

"*Take them...It's all yours!*"

Thereupon, unable to hold back his excitement, Safwan exclaimed:

"No heart other than a Prophet's can be that generous", before following it up with the Word of Faith and becoming a Muslim.[17]

Once he returned to his tribe, he was quick to declare:

"Run, my people, to accept Islam…for Muhammad donates abundantly without the tiniest fear of poverty and need!" (Muslim, Fadail, 57-58; Ahmad, III, 107)

Once, another person came by and asked something from the Prophet ﷺ who had nothing to give at the time. But the Prophet ﷺ, nonetheless, told the man to find a loan, assuring him that he would pay it off on his behalf. (Haythami, X, 242)[18]

In the spirit of his ancestor Ibrahim عليه السلام, the Prophet of Grace ﷺ would never have a meal alone, without guests. He would either sponsor the debts of the deceased, or find suitable sponsors, refusing to perform their funeral *salat* before their dues were paid off.

"*A generous person is closer to Allah, to Paradise and to people, and distant to the flames of Hell. But a miser is distant to Allah, to Paradise and to people and close to Hellfire*," he has stated. (Tirmidhi, Birr, 40/1961)

In another hadith he states:

"*Two traits never come together in a true Muslim: Miserliness and bad morals…*" (Tirmidhi, Birr, 41/1962)

17. Wâqidî, *Magazi,* Beirut 1989, II, 854-855.
18. Also see, Abû Dawud, Harâj, 33-35/3055; Ibn Hibbân, *Sahîh,* Beirut, 1993, XIV, 262-264.

The Piety of the Prophet of Allah ﷺ

He was indisputably the most pious among all people. Common for him was his prayer to the Almighty to be granted with piety, that is, with *taqwa*:

"*Allah…Grant my self piety and refine it…for You are the One to refine it; its Helper and Lord.*" (Muslim, Dhikr, 73)

"*Allah…I plea to You to give me guidance, piety, chastity and richness of heart.*" (Muslim, Dhikr, 72)

Piety compelled him to live a poor life. Mother Aisha reports that there was never a time that the Prophet ﷺ got to enjoy as little as a barley bread on two consecutive days, and on another account, a wheat bread on three consecutive days. (Bukhari, Ayman, 22; Muslim, Zuhd, 20-22; Ibn Majah, At'imah, 48)

In encouraging his *ummah* to take up a life of piety, he is known to have said:

"*Closest to me among people are the pious who, wherever they are, uphold their piety for Allah.*" (Ahmad, V, 235; Haythami, IX, 22)

"*My friends, without a doubt, are the pious.*" (Abu Dawud, Fitan, 1/4242)

"*Wherever you are fear Allah with piety and immediately follow up a bad deed with a good to efface it. Treat people with the best of morals…*" (Tirmidhi, Birr, 55/1987)

As for the way to attain true *taqwa*:

"*…the rank of true taqwa remains out of reach, so long as one does not abandon certain permissible things from fear of straying toward the impermissible.*" (Tirmidhi, Qiyamah, 19/2451; Ibn Majah, Zuhd, 24)

Supremacy, for him, was not something exercised by whites against blacks, nor nations against one another; it much rather came through piety. (Ahmad, V, 158)

A splendid enunciation of piety comes from Isa (as), in his answer to a person who once asked him:

"Tell me, the teacher of goodness and virtue, how one becomes pious in the sight of the Lord."

"*It is easy*", responded Isa (as). "*You first become attached to the Lord with a deep love, then perform good deeds to the best of your ability and feel mercy for the entire Children of Adam just as you feel mercy for yourself.*"

He then added:

"*...and do not do to others what you would not wish upon yourself. Only then will you become pious in the sight of Lord.*"[19]

Omar (ra) once asked Ubayy ibn Qab (ra) the meaning of *taqwa.*

"Have you ever treaded a thorny path?" asked Ubayy (ra).

"Yes."

"So what did you do?"

"I lifted my clothes and focused on my every step not to be spiked by the thorns," replied Omar (ra).

"Such is *taqwa*," Ubayy (ra) thereupon stated.[20]

Spiritually closest to the Blessed Prophet ﷺ are the pious. The below account is provided by Muadh ibn Jabal (ra):

19. Ahmad, *az-Zuhd*, p. 59.
20. Ibn Kathîr, *Tafsîru'l-Qur'âni'l-Azîm*, Beirut 1988, I, 42.

"Sending me off to Yemen as governor, the Messenger of Allah ﷺ accompanied me to the outskirts of Medina to farewell me. I was astride, and he walking by my side. After giving me some advice, he said:

'*Who knows, Muadh, you might not be able to see me again after this year. Bu perhaps you will visit my Masjid over there and my grave...*'

Hearing those words, coupled with the grief of separating from *the* friend, reduced me to tears.

'*Do not cry*', consoled the Messenger of Allah ﷺ. Then turning his gaze toward Medina, he said:

'*Closest to me among people are the pious who, wherever they are, uphold their piety for Allah.*'"[21]

The Prophet of Allah's ﷺ Life of Abstinence

Time came when all the neighboring lands willingly pledged allegiance to the Blessed Prophet ﷺ, rendering him the master of all Arabia. In spite of the lavishness he could have certainly indulged in, he instead chose to continue his simple life. He confessed he exercised no power over anything and that everything was in the hand of might of Allah, glory unto Him. Time came when riches began flowing his way. Caravans loaded with lavish treasures poured wealth into the streets of Medina. Donating them all to the needy, he held fast to his illustrious life of abstinence, that is of *zuhd*, saying:

21. Ahmad, V, 235; Haythamî, *Majmau'z-Zawâid*, Beirut, 1988, IX, 22.

"*If I had gold as great as Mount Uhud, apart for my debts, I would not store it more than three days.*" (Bukhari, Tamanni, 2; Muslim, Zakat, 31)

Days would go by without there being a fire lit, in the house of the Prophet ﷺ for cooking; and more often than not, he would sleep on an empty stomach. (Ahmad, VI, 217; Ibn Sad, I, 405)

Omar ؓ had once arrived at the Prophet's house. He took a look around the room; it was bare except for a straw mattress woven with date leaves, against which the Prophet ﷺ was laying. The dry straw mattress had left its imprints on his blessed skin. In a corner there also stood a cupful of barley flour, hanging beside which, by a nail, was an old water bottle made out of leather. And that was it! That was the entire wealth of a man, to whose will the entire Arabian Peninsula had surrendered. Omar ؓ let out a deep sigh, and was suddenly overwhelmed with tears by the touching sight.

"*Why are you crying?*" asked the Noble Prophet ﷺ.

"Why would I not?" replied Omar ؓ. "The Caesars and Khousraus swim in worldly pleasures while the Prophet of Allah sleeps on a parched mattress..."

The Prophet ﷺ then consoled the aching heart of his dear friend:

"*Do not cry, Omar... Wouldn't you want them to have the world with all its pleasures and us the Hereafter?*"[22]

Again, in reaction to a similar incident, he once said:

22. See, Ahmad, II, 298; Tabarânî, *al-Mu'jamu'l-Kabîr,* prepared and published by Hamdi Abdülmajid as-Salafî, Beirut, Dâru Ihyâi't-Turathi'l-Arabî, X, 162.

"What is it to me of the world? My state in the world is like that of a wayfarer who on a hot summer day momentarily shades under a tree then continues along his journey."[23]

Repetitiously, with the stirring anxiety of being called into account for worldly gains in the Hereafter, the Prophet ﷺ would pray:

"Allah...Make me live a poor man, die a poor man and resurrect me with the poor!" (Tirmidhi, Zuhd, 37/2352; Ibn Majah, Zuhd, 7)

Though under the amnesty of being guaranteed with Paradise, prophets will also be called into account for their received blessings in the world and whether or not they communicated the Divine Message, a circumstance verified by the Quran:

"Most certainly then We will question those to whom (the messengers) were sent, and most certainly We will also question the messengers." (Araf, 6)

❁

Expressions like *zuhd, taqwa* and *ihsan* are different words that in effect convey the same meaning. The common aim pervading these concepts that comprise also the gist of Sufi training, is to guide the heart to peace and tranquility by virtue of shackling the insidious desires of the self and developing the inner capacity for the spiritual, which in turn is the articulation of *qalb'us-salim*, a heart of purity, imperative to become a true servant of the Real.

23. Tirmidhî, Zuhd, 44/2377; Ibn Mâjah, Zuhd, 3; Ahmad, I, 301.

The Courtesy of the Prophet of Allah ﷺ

To understand the maturity the refined heart of the Blessed Prophet ﷺ had attained, it would suffice for one to recall the time when, seeing a man spit on the ground, his gracious face turned red and was reduced to stillness. Only after some Companions rushed to cover the spit with some sand was he able to move on.

Constantly commanding others to take care of the way they dressed and disliking an unkempt approach in clothing, the Prophet ﷺ would at the same time not condone unkempt hair and beards. Once, while in the *Masjid*, a man had arrived with messy hair and beard. The Prophet ﷺ signaled at him to fix his look; and after he did as he had been told, the Messenger of Allah ﷺ declared:

"*Now doesn't that look better than going around like Satan with unkempt hair?*" (Muwatta', Shaar, 7)[24]

On another occasion, the Prophet again saw another man with a muddled appearance. Astonished, he said:

"*Why doesn't he wash his hair and look after it?*"

Seeing another with dirty clothes, yet at another time, he pronounced the need for Muslims to be clean and tidy, with the words:

"*Can not that man find any water to clean his clothes?*" (Abu Dawud, Libas, 14/4062; Nasai, Zinat, 60)

At another time, to a man who had arrived at his presence in an untidy manner, the Noble Prophet ﷺ asked how his

24. Bayhakî, *Shuabu'l-Imân*, Beirut 1990, V, 225

financial status was. And when the man confessed to being well-to-do, the Messenger of Allah ﷺ cautioned him:

"*...then allow Allah to see the trace of His blessings on you!*" (Abu Dawud, Libas, 14/4063; Nasai, Zinat, 54; Ahmad, IV, 137)

Another similar hadith states:

"*Allah likes to see the trace of the blessings on the servant whom He gives.*" (Tirmidhi, Adab, 54/2819; Ahmad, II, 311)

The exemplary character of the Prophet ﷺ marks the pinnacle of mercy, courtesy and an elegance of heart. Even to a crude Beduoin shouting vulgarly and repetitiously from behind him:

"Muhammad, over here," he still knew how to say,

"*Yes, what can I do for you?*" and thus respond to a shameless rudeness with supreme courtesy.[25]

Inspired by an extreme sense of courtesy, the Prophet of Grace ﷺ would always serve his guests with his own hands. (Bayhaki, *Shuab*, VI, 518, VII, 436)

Even during his childhood, he was never known to transgress the bounds of courtesy and quarrel with anyone.

Together with exuding an enormous depth of courtesy in his own person, the Blessed Prophet ﷺ had also reared his family in a way compliant with the same supreme morals.

Providing a beautiful testimony indeed is the experience below of Hasan ؓ, the Noble Prophet's grandson:

25. See, Muslim, Nudhur, 8; Abu Dâwûd, Aymân, 21/3316; Tirmidhî, Zuhd, 50; Ahmad, IV, 239.

Once having circumambulated the Kabah and performed two *rakahs* of salat by the Site of Ibrahim, Hasan ﵁ lifted his hands aloft and touchingly prayed:

"*Allah...a small and weak servant has come by to Your door. O Allah...a helpless slave begs by Your sill. Allah...a beggar has come, Your vulnerable slave...*"

Hasan ﵁ then left following the poignant supplication and on the way stumbled across a few poor people trying to placate their hunger with a loaf of bread. To raise their spirits he greeted the crowd and went next to them. Cheered by his considerate approach, they in turn invited Hasan ﵁ to join in their humble feast.

So the Grandson of the Prophet modestly sat with them and said:

"Had I have known this bread was not charity I would not have hesitated to eat with you." Then, to again comfort the poor folk, Hasan ﵁ stood and courteously said:

"Come on, let's go to our place!"

There he fed them and donned them in new clothes, moreover putting some money in their pockets before cheerfully seeing them off. By the time the encounter was over, he had won over all their hearts. (See: Abshihi, al-Mustatraf, Beirut 1986, I, 31)

What a magnificent indication such courtesy and elegance at the same time provides for the manner in which the Creator gazes at humankind through with the Gaze of Mercy and Benevolence.

Still, there is more to the kindness of Hasan ﵁.

Strolling through the vineyards of Medina once, Hasan ﵁ saw a black slave helping himself to some of the bread he was holding in his hand, while feeding some of it to a dog waiting before him.

Instantly spellbound by the manifestation of the Divine Name *Rahman*, the Merciful, in kindhearted deed of the slave, Hasan ﷺ asked him the reason as to why he would do such a thing, though the slave was to shy to look at Hasan ﷺ in the face.

"Who are you, lad?" asked thereupon Hasan ﷺ.

"I am a servant of Aban, son of Othman ﷺ," the slave replied.

"Then to whom does this vineyard belong?"

"To Aban..."

With the wish of becoming closer to the seemingly ordinary slave who discernibly was a beloved of Allah and a sultan of the realm of the spiritual, Hasan ﷺ said:

"Do not leave...I will return in a moment!"

He then hurriedly went next to Aban, the owner of the vineyard, and purchased both the vineyard and the slave of him. He then arrived by the side of the slave once more:

"Lad...I have purchased you."

"Very well," said the lad respectfully. "Then it is my duty to obey Allah and His Messenger, and you..."

Becoming emotional all the more upon hearing these words, Hasan ﷺ had grown even greater in his admiration for the young lad, owing to his sincere loyalty. To reciprocate the beauty of heart possessed by the slave that had sent him into the depths of a profound stir of emotion, Hasan ﷺ pronounced:

"For Allah's sake, from now on you are free...and the vineyard is yours as present!" (Ibn Manzur, Muhtasaru Tarihi Dimashq, VII, 25)

The Manners and Haya[26] of the Prophet of Allah ﷺ

The Noble Prophet ﷺ never spoke at the top of his voice. In public, he would walk composedly, always with a smile on his face. Given someone uttered a coarse, offensive word next to him, the Blessed Prophet ﷺ would never put him down in public; besides, since his facial expressions persistently reflected his inner state, people would be tentative in what they did or spoke next to him. Owing to his *haya*, he is never known to have laughed loudly, always content instead with a warm smile. On the words of the Companions, he was shier than a maiden enshrouded in her veil.

He has expressed in a hadith:

"*Haya is from iman* (faith in Allah), *and whosoever has it is in Paradise. Lack of it is from a hardness of the heart; and a heart of stone is in Hellfire.*" (Bukhari, Iman, 16)

"*Haya and iman go hand in hand...when one leaves, the other follows!*" (Tabarani, Awsat, VIII, 174; Bayhaqi, Shuab, VI, 140)

"*Vulgar words incur nothing but shame, while haya and manners adorn wherever they enter.*" (Muslim, Birr, 78; Abu Dawud, Jihad, 1)

26. *Haya* does not fully translate into English. Though the term does invoke *embarrassment* or *introversion* it is not so in the truest sense. *Haya*, much rather, denotes an inner state withdrawal, from a fear of Allah, a state of mind, that results in restraining behavior or actions that would otherwise conflict with the spirit of Divine Command. (translator)

True *haya* is acquired through a remembrance of death, a means to purge the heart of the love of the world. The Prophet of Grace ﷺ continuously advised his Companions to develop a sense of *haya* for the Almighty as appropriate to His Majesty. At one time, when they appreciatively expressed that they had *haya* for their Lord, the Prophet ﷺ explained real *haya* as protecting all parts of the body from the impermissible and never taking the thought of death out of the mind. The desire of the Hereafter, he then continued, necessitated the abandonment of the love of the world and that such were the only people filled with a proper sense of *haya* for their Lord. (Tirmidhi, Qiyamah, 24/2458)

The Messenger of Allah ﷺ would never stare inquisitively at anyone in the face. His gaze spent greater time fixed on the ground than it did at the skies. Stemming from a supreme character endowed with such *haya*, never would he use people's mistakes against them.

As conveyed by Aisha ؓ, whenever the Prophet ﷺ was delivered with a word he was not fond of, he would not react by saying:

"Why is so and so saying these things?" but instead by remarking "*why are some people saying these things?*" (Abu Dawud, Adab, 5/4788)

And sometimes, to impart a feeling of dislike for certain inappropriate behavior, he would caution them in the most sophisticated manner, saying:

"*Why am I seeing such and such things committed?*",[27] as if to figuratively turn the blame on himself.

27. Buhârî, Menâkıb 25, Eymân 3; Müslim, Salât, 119; İbn-i Hibbân, IV, 534.

Virtually quivering not to break anyone's heart even when counseling them, the Prophet of Excellence ﷺ was thus a lofty tower of compassion.

Having imbibed such Prophetic morals, Mawlana Rumi, that illustrious friend of the Truth, swathes abstract realities in concrete words when he says:

"'*What is Iman?' asked my reason to my heart. Whispering into the ear of my reason, my heart replied, 'Iman is but manners (adab).*"

The Courage of the Prophet of Allah ﷺ

Nowhere seen to give in to fear and anxiety throughout his life, it is inconceivable to even try to imagine a hero greater than the Messenger of Allah ﷺ. Patient and persevering in times of extraordinary dread, he would never act inappropriately, like most tend to do when under the spell of fright.

Reciting but the two *ayah* from Chapter Yasin below, he had bravely and indifferently walked through the ranks of those waiting to slay him:

اِنَّا جَعَلْنَا فِيٓ اَعْنَاقِهِمْ اَغْلَالًا فَهِىَ اِلَى الْاَذْقَانِ فَهُمْ مُقْمَحُونَ وَجَعَلْنَا مِنْ بَيْنِ اَيْدِيهِمْ سَدًّا وَمِنْ خَلْفِهِمْ سَدًّا فَاَغْشَيْنَاهُمْ فَهُمْ لَا يُبْصِرُونَ

"We have put yokes round their necks right up to their chins, so that their heads are forced up (and they cannot see).

And We have put a bar in front of them and a bar behind them, and further, We have covered them up; so that they cannot see." (Yasin, 8-9)

Ali ﷺ recounts:

"When the Battle of Badr was continuing with all its vigor, we were taking refuge behind the Messenger of Allah ﷺ. He was by far our bravest…he would always be positioned closest to the enemy ranks." (Ahmad, I, 86)

A similar report is given by Bara ﷺ. with regard to the Blessed Prophet's ﷺ courage:

"By Allah, whenever the battle got fierce, we would seek the shelter of the Messenger of Allah ﷺ. We would regard the next most courageous as he, courageous enough to stand in the same line as him." (Muslim, Jihad, 79)

For *i'la-i kalimatullah*, that is to raise the word of Allah and render His religion the highest, he would always be in the frontline of battle. During the Battle of Hunayn, despite the initial disarray of the Muslim army, he proved he had lost none of his resolve as he lunged into the center of the enemy lines, charging his mule further into their core, raising thereby the courage of his Companions, until with Divine assistance, they were able to turn the tide and claim victory. (Muslim, Jihad, 76-81)

He would say:

"By Allah under whose Power and Will I abide, I would dearly love to fight for the sake of Allah and be martyred; then be revived to fight once more and be martyred again, and again…" (Muslim, Imarah, 103)

The Gentleness of the Prophet of Allah ﷺ

The Blessed Prophet ﷺ was the gentlest among his peers (Muslim, Hajj, 137), which brings to mind the testimony of Aisha (r.a.):

"There was nobody with more beautiful morals than the Messenger of Allah ﷺ. Whenever someone from his family or among his friends called him, he always responded in the politest way. It was owing to his sublime morals that Allah, glory unto Him, revealed the verse:

'**And you stand on an exalted standard of character.**' (al-Qalam, 4)" (Wahidi, p.463)

Throughout his life the Noble Messenger ﷺ never sought personal revenge, habitually opting to forgive instead.

Aisha (r.a.), again, elaborates the gentleness of the morals of the Prophet ﷺ along the following lines:

"He never humiliated anyone…neither did he respond to evil except with forgiveness and lenience. He always stood remote from evil. Never has he taken personal revenge from anyone. There is neither a slave nor a servant, even an animal he has handled unjustly."[28]

The words below, reminiscent of the Blessed Prophet, belong to Anas (r.a.):

"I have never touched a satin or silk softer than the hands of the Messenger of Allah ﷺ. Neither have I smelt a fragrance sweeter than his. I served him for exactly ten years. He was never frustrated with me; not even once did he say 'phew'. Not only did he ever ask 'why did you do this' for something I did,

28. Bkz. Müslim, Fedâil, 79

he did not ever remark 'should not have you done this' for something that I did not." (Bukhari, Sawm 53, Manaqib 23; Muslim, Fadail 82)

The Prophet ﷺ once praised a companion, commenting:

"*You have two traits Allah is fond of: Gentleness (hilm) and discretion (taannii).*" (Muslim, Iman, 25, 26)

A Bedouin, at one time, had urinated in the Mosque of Medina. The Companions immediately began rebuking him, until the Blessed Prophet ﷺ intervened:

"*It's best you leave the man alone. Just pour a bucket of water over where he has urinated...for you have been sent to make things easy, not to cause difficulty.*"

He then benignly explained to the Bedouin the importance of mosques and the manners to have therein.

Anas ؓ says:

"I was walking with the Messenger of Allah ﷺ. He was wearing a mantle made of Najran fabric, with thick and rigid edges. A Bedouin then caught up with the Prophet of Allah ﷺ and tugged the mantle from behind so forcefully that the edge of the mantle, as I saw it, became par with his neck. The Bedouin then shouted:

'Muhammad! Order them to give me some of what you have with you of the goods that belong to Allah!'

The Messenger of Allah simply turned around and smiled at the man, before ensuring he received some goods." (Bukhari, Khumus 19, Libas 18, Adab 68; Muslim, Zakat 128)

His remarkable success in the Call was in fact through the blessings of such magnificent conduct, a maturity of the Prophet ﷺ described by the Almighty as:

فَبِمَا رَحْمَةٍ مِنَ اللّٰهِ لِنْتَ لَهُمْ وَلَوْ كُنْتَ فَظًّا غَلِيظَ الْقَلْبِ لَانْفَضُّوا مِنْ حَوْلِكَ

"Thus it is due to mercy from Allah that you deal with them gently, and had you been rough, hard hearted, they would certainly have dispersed from around you…" (Ali Imran, 159)

Without a shadow of a doubt, the people of the Age of Ignorance had melted like a candle to the flame that was the gentle, virtuous and lenient character of the Noble Messenger ﷺ; and saved from the uncompromising wilderness in which they were trapped, they became moths spinning around that Light, compassionately aching for the good of humanity.

The Mercy and Compassion of the Prophet of Allah ﷺ

The Prophet of Mercy ﷺ states in a hadith:

"*Allah, glory unto Him, the Rahman, has mercy for those who are merciful. Show mercy and compassion for those on Earth so that you will be shown mercy and compassion by those in the Heavens.*" (Tirmidhi, Birr, 16/1924)

The profound mercy the Messenger of Allah ﷺ was imbued with becomes conspicuous, among other selfless deeds, in his giving permission to a mother to shorten her *salat* given she has her toddler incessantly crying by her side, and no less in his many nights of praying, with teary eyes, for the wellbeing of his *ummah* and his sacrifice of his entire time for the salvation of mankind from Hellfire.

Since he was sent as a mercy for the entire realm of being, the compassion of the Blessed Prophet ﷺ had encompassed every single creature. Asked, on one occasion, to curse the disbelievers, he instead replied:

"*I have not been sent to Earth to curse…for I am a Prophet of Mercy*." (Muslim, Fadail, 126; Tirmidhi, Daawat, 118)

When he went to the town of Taif to convey the call of Islam, he was stoned by its ignorant and selfish community. The Angel of the Mountains, accompanied by Jibril, then came to the Blessed Prophet ﷺ, avowing to:

"…strike these two mountains together and lay waste to their existence," if he wished. But the Prophet ﷺ did not.

"*No*", he said. "*I only wish that the Almighty will send forth from their progeny a generation who will worship none other than Allah and will ascribe none as partners to Him.*" (Bukhari, Bad'ul-Khalq, 7; Muslim, Jihad, 111)

For the dwellers of Taif, the Thaqif, who had expelled him from their town amid unspeakable insults and who had held out until the ninth year of Hegira at the expense of many Muslim casualties, the Noble Prophet ﷺ prayed persistently:

"*O Allah…Grant guidance to the tribe of Thaqif…Send them to us of their own accord*", until in the end, they arrived at Medina to enter the folds of Islam, by their own will. (Ibn Hisham, IV, 134; Tirmidhi, Manaqib, 73/3942)

Abu Usayd ؓ once came to the Prophet ﷺ with some prisoners of war he had taken captive at Bahrain. The Blessed Prophet ﷺ saw a female captive crying and so he asked for the reason why she was.

"That man sold my son", she complained.

"*Did you?*" the Prophet of Grace ﷺ inquired, turning his gaze to Abu Usayd ﷺ.

"Yes", responded Abu Usayd ﷺ.

"*To whom...?*"

"...To the Abs Clan."

The Messenger of Allah ﷺ thereupon commanded the Companion to:

"*Mount your horse, go and return with the lady's son!*"[29]

As exemplified by the following account, the Prophet's ﷺ benevolence was of a universal character. He once stated, with the Companions by his side:

"*By Allah, under whose Power I abide, you will not enter Paradise until you are compassionate.*"

"But, Messenger of Allah, we are all compassionate", the Companions commented.

"*Compassion is not simply that you nurture for one another. Rather it is something that extends to entire creation; yes...to creation in its entirety.*" (Hakim, IV, 185/7310)

The Lenience of the Prophet of Allah ﷺ

Allah, glory unto Him, loves to forgive. Allah pledges to accept the repentance of a servant, who repents with a sincere feeling of remorse for the wrongdoings committed; and being

29. Ali al-Muttaqî al-Hindî, *Kanzu'l-Ummâl,* Beirut 1985, IV, 176/10044.

a Bountiful Forgiver, He also encourages His servants to adopt the same approach towards others.

The condition of being forgiven is remorse, as well as abiding by the Commands of the Creator and steering clear of the impermissible thereafter. The most splendid instances of forgiving others are to be found in the life of the Prophet of Mercy ﷺ. One recalls, first and foremost, how, on the day of the Conquest of Mecca, for the sake of the splendor of *tawhid*, he forgave Hind, the woman who had fiercely ripped her teeth into the severed lungs of Hamza during the grim Battle of Uhud.

Habbar ibn Aswad was among the most vicious enemies of Islam. Spitefully poking, with his spear, the camel on which Zaynab ؓ was astride right before her migration to Medina, she had caused the daughter of the Noble Prophet ﷺ to fall of, consequently leaving her bloody and bruised, and above all, with a miscarriage of the baby she was pregnant with at the time. Most regrettable was the fact that the wound would eventually end up as the cause of her death a short time later. Habbar was the culprit of many malevolent crimes alike. He had fled on the Day of the Conquest of Mecca, eluding all attempts of being captured. A while later he tentatively appeared in Medina at the presence of the Prophet of Grace ﷺ, while he was sitting with the Companions. All he did was to announce he had become Muslim. Not only did the Prophet ﷺ forgive him, he moreover prohibited all others from even abusing Habbar and throwing him insults. (Waqidi, II, 857-858)

Another distinguished foe of Islam was Iqrimah, the son of the notorious Abu Jahl. He had taken flight to Yemen following the triumphant arrival of the Believers in Mecca.

After a great toil, Iqrimah was persuaded by his wife to seek the amnesty of the Noble Messenger ﷺ, in whose presence he appeared a short time later, but this time as a Muslim.

"*Welcome, you wandering cavalier*," the Gracious Prophet ﷺ greeted Iqrimah gleefully; and concealing his bygone malicious deeds against the Muslims, he pardoned him. (Tirmidhi, Isti'zan, 34/2735)

The Messenger of Allah ﷺ would incessantly pray:

"*Allah…Forgive my ummah, for they do not know*." (Ibn Majah, Manasiq, 56; Ahmad, IV, 14)

Immediately after accepting Islam, Sumamah ibn Usal, the leader of Yamamah, severed all commercial ties with Mecca, which hitherto depended on Yamamah for nearly all her provisions. Finding themselves all of a sudden in the throes of scarcity, the shocked Meccans implored the Blessed Prophet ﷺ to intervene. Writing a letter to Sumamah, the Prophet of Mercy ﷺ counseled him to continue trade with Meccans.[30]

Yet it was these very idolaters of Mecca who had put up a stern three year boycott against the Muslims, inflicting the Believers with incredible torment. But the Blessed Prophet ﷺ still had room to forgive even that.

What's more, during the seventh year of Hegira in the wake of the Capture of Khaybar, the Noble Prophet ﷺ aided the depleted Meccans, who were battling fierce famine and scarcity, with supplies of gold, barley and date seeds. Accepting

30. İbn-i Abdilberr, *el-İstîâb,* Kâhire ts., I, 214-215; İbn-i Esîr, *Üsdü'l-Gâbe,* Kâhire 1970, I, 295.

the aid, Abu Sufyan distributed it among the Meccan needy, as he remarked with gratitude:

"May Allah award our Cousin for looking out for his relatives..." (Yaqubi, II, 56)

Their hearts growing tender through such acts of magnanimity, the Meccans soon found themselves wholeheartedly and unreservedly accepting Islam.

The Blessed Messenger ﷺ even forgave a cavalry captured at Hudaybiya, who had confessed their intentions to assassinate him. (Muslim, Jihad, 132, 133)

A woman, following the Conquest of Khaybar, had contaminated the Noble Prophet's ﷺ food with poison. The Messenger of Allah ﷺ realized the food had been poisoned just as he was taking a piece of the meat toward his mouth. Despite the woman admitting to being the one with the vicious plan, the Noble Prophet ﷺ still forgave her regardless. (Bukhari, Tibb, 55; Muslim, Salam, 43)

Through Revelation, the Prophet ﷺ had found out about Labid, the Jew who had put an agonizing spell on him, and those who had encouraged Labid to resort to the sinister act. But the Noble Messenger ﷺ never even once mentioned Labid's misdemeanor and never held the crime against him. He never sought revenge by killing Labid and his fellow Jews of Banu Zurayq.[31]

The Quran had after all advised:

"Hold to forgiveness; command what is right; But turn away from the ignorant." (al-Araf, 199)

31. See, Ibn Sad, II, 197; Bukhari, Tıbb, 47, 49; Muslim, Salâm, 43; Nasâî, Tahrîm, 20; Ahmad, IV, 367, VI, 57; Aynî, XXI, 282.

The wise, who through love have striven to pave a path of nearness with the Light of Being ﷺ, and who have therefore been able to receive a share of his forgiving nature, have likewise always been forgiving, with the ambition of incurring Divine Mercy. One only needs to recall the words of Hallaj Mansur while being stoned:

"My Lord…Forgive the stoners before You forgive me…"

The Prophet of Allah's ﷺ Observance of Neighbor's Rights

The Prophet of Mercy ﷺ demanded utmost sensitivity towards observing the rights of neighbors.

"*So many times did Jibril repeat his advice to treat the neighbor with goodness,*" said the Prophet ﷺ "*that I nearly thought neighbors would become the inheritors of one another.*" (Bukhari, Adab, 28; Muslim, Birr, 140-141)

And in another Hadith he states:

"*A neighbor, who is a nonbeliever, has one right. A Muslim neighbor has two. A Muslim, who moreover is a relative, has three.*"[32]

Staring through a neighbor's window, causing discomfort through the smell of food and engaging in conduct to their displeasure are among violations of the rights of neighbors.

Thus would say the Light of Being ﷺ:

"*The best neighbor in the sight of Allah is he who is of benefit to his neighbor.*" (Tirmidhi, Birr, 28)

32. Suyûtî, *al-Jâmiu's-Saghîr,* Egypt 1321, I, 146.

"*He is not a Muslim who sleeps on a full stomach while his neighbor is hungry.*" (Hakim, II, 15/2166a)

Abu Dharr Ghifari ﷺ recounts:

"Whenever I was about to cook food, the Messenger of Allah ﷺ would tell me to add extra water and give some of it to my neighbor." (Ibn Majah, Atimah, 58)

Considering Abu Dharr ﷺ was among the poorest of the Companions, it thus means that not even poorness is a valid excuse to evade donation.

Narrated by Abu Hurayra ﷺ, one day the Blessed Prophet ﷺ stated:

"*By Allah he would not have believed, by Allah he would not have believed, by Allah he would not have believed...*"

"Who would not have believed, Messenger of Allah?" asked the Companions present.

"*He*", said the Prophet ﷺ "*whose neighbor does not feel safe from his harm.*" (Bukhari, Adab, 29; Muslim, Iman, 73; Tirmidhi, Qiyamat, 60)

According to another account:

"*One from whose harm his neighbor feels insecure shall not enter Paradise.*" (Muslim, Iman, 73)

The Prophet of Allah's ﷺ Treatment of the Poor

Renowned for his benevolence for and caring intimacy with the poor, the lonely and the widowed (Bukhari, Nafaqat, 1; Muslim, Zuhd, 41-42) the Prophet of Grace ﷺ would treat them with utmost care as if to compensate for their lack of financial welfare.

Abu Said ؓ narrates:

"I was seated with a group of poor men from among the *Muhajirun*. Some of them, without adequate clothing to even cover their bodies, were ducking under the shadows of others for cover. Someone was reciting us some Quran. Meanwhile the Messenger of Allah ﷺ appeared all of a sudden and waited awhile, standing. Upon his arrival, the person reciting the Quran stopped his recital. Then the Messenger of Allah ﷺ greeted us and asked:

'*What are you doing?*'

'*He is our teacher*,' we said. '*He reads us the Quran and we lend ear to the Book of Allah.*'

'*Thanks be to Allah who has created, among my ummah, those I have been command to bear patient with*,'[33] then said the Prophet of Allah ﷺ.

Then with supreme modesty, the Messenger of Allah ﷺ sat amongst us. Signaling with his finger, he said:

'*Form a circle like this...*'

33. It is an allusion to, "**And withhold yourself with those who call on their Lord morning and evening desiring His goodwill, and let not your eyes pass from them, desiring the beauties of this world's life; and do not follow him whose heart We have made unmindful to Our remembrance, and he follows his low desires and his case is one in which due bounds are exceeded.**" (al-Kahf, 28), where Allah, glory unto Him, commands the Prophet ﷺ with patience and perseverance, alongside the weak and the poor to have been the first to enter Islam, at the face of possible hardships that may befall them, and to treat them with utmost sensitivity.

All of us, thereupon, formed a circle around the Messenger ﷺ, facing him. That was when he gave us the following good news:

'*Glad tidings to you, the poor folk of Muhajirun...I give you the good news of a full light in the Hereafter. You will enter Paradise half a day before the rich...a half a day that equals the sum of five hundred years on Earth!*'" (Abu Dawud, Ilm, 13/3666)

At one time a tribe arrived in Medina, without anything to wear on their feet, emaciated from hunger and the sweltering heat. Their moving sight touched the Prophet of Grace ﷺ to his core; he suddenly grew pale. By getting Bilal ؓ to recite the *adhan*, he gathered the Companions, and made them aware of the plight of the visitors. He was relieved somewhat after some among them, with means, volunteered to aid the troubled tribe. (Muslim, Zakat, 69-70; Ahmad, IV, 358, 361)

The Noble Prophet's ﷺ life thus abounds in fascinating instances of profound compassion.

"*Aisha, do not refuse the poor, even if it be with half a date. Love the poor and seek nearness with them so that Allah will draw you near on the Day of Judgment*", the Noble Messenger ﷺ would constantly advise his wife. (Tirmidhi, Zuhd, 37/2352)

Recounting the following is Abbad ibn Shurahbil ؓ:

"A while ago, I entered a field in Medina, having fallen poor and looking for something to eat. I pulled out some grains, ate some and filled some into my bag. Out of nowhere the owner of the garden appeared; grabbing hold of me, he beat me, seized possession of my bag and moreover took me to the Messenger of Allah ﷺ to file a complaint.

'*You did not teach him when he was ignorant, neither did you feed him when he was hungry*', the Messenger of Allah ﷺ told the field owner, asking him to return me my bag.

The Messenger of Allah ﷺ then gave me enough supplies. (Abu Dawud, Jihad, 85/2620-2621; Nasai, Qudat, 21)

Islam demands an investigation first of the source of a crime, then a paramount effort to correct the criminal. From this perspective, penalties in Islamic Law are akin to the reprimand of children by their parents. The aim is not to banish the criminal, but to regain him back into society.

The Prophet of Allah's ﷺ Treatment of Captives and Servants

The mercy of the Blessed Prophet ﷺ generously extended to prisoners of war, where he would order those around him to treat them with care. An evocative testimony is offered by Abu Aziz, brother of Musab ibn Umayr ؓ:

"I too had fallen prisoner in the aftermath of the Battle of Badr and was handed to a group of *Ansar*. The Prophet's ﷺ command to treat the prisoners well was made known to everyone but the pains taken by the Ansar was something out of the ordinary. Day and night, they would give their share of bread to me, making do themselves with mere dates. Embarrassed, I would hand the bread back to one of them, only to have it returned to me, without anyone of them laying a hand on it." (Haythami, VI, 86; Ibn Hisham, II, 288)

The Messenger of Allah ﷺ aimed toward abolishing the long-lasting system of slavery and took great steps towards its realization. Encouraging, at every given opportunity, to set a slave free, he declared the act to be a great deed of worship. Freeing a slave became the foremost step toward redemption, whenever a Muslim committed a wrongdoing. With his encouragement, Abu Bakr ﷺ, his closest friend, spent a great portion of his wealth in the way of freeing slaves.

The Prophet of Mercy ﷺ on one occasion witnessed Abu Dharr ﷺ unknowingly maltreat his slave. Upset, he warned the Companion, remarking:

"*It seems you are still following the customs of Ignorance*", before continuing:

"*Do not harm what Allah has created. If the slave does not suit your temperament, then set him free. Do not burden him with more than he can handle; and if you do, then help him.*" (Bukhari, Iman, 22; Muslim, Ayman, 38; Abu Dawud, Adab, 123-124)

A man had arranged a marriage between two of his slaves, only to have a change of heart, trying to separate them a while later. The male slave reported the affair to the Prophet ﷺ who told the slave owner to:

"*Keep out of it…you exercise no rights over their marriage and divorce.*" (Ibn Majah, Talaq, 31; Tabarani, Kabir, XI, 300)

Faced with daunting responsibilities of the kinds mentioned, the Companions in time ended up preferring setting their slaves free over keeping them, which in due course culminated in the abolishment of the whole system as it now stands today; that is to say, it was again Islam that lifted the chains of slavery, a side effect of warfare and an enduring part of the history of mankind, from the neck of humanity.

Islam has always advised the slave owner to clothe and feed the slave from what he would see fit to clothe and feed himself, not to overload the slave with more than he can bare and to attend to all his needs. Freeing a slave has thus persistently been encouraged, for a Muslim, as a deed of virtue and an ultimate means of salvation. It has brought such rights for slaves that observing them has virtually rendered refraining from purchasing a slave preferable over owning one; such that owning a slave has practically come bear a similar meaning to becoming enslaved.

The words below of the Messenger of Allah ﷺ, one of his last, deserve a good reflection:

"*Be attentive to salat and salat especially...Fear Allah for those under your care.*" (Abu Dawud, Adab, 123-124/5156; Ibn Majah, Wasaya, 1)

Thus the Blessed Prophet ﷺ effectively closed the gates to slavery as far as circumstances permitted, and in turn fully opened its doors of exit, whereby aiding people under such yoke to attain their freedom has been encouraged at every given opportunity. Could there be a better method than that to end slavery?

The accounts below should suffice to get a clearer vision of the position to which Islam elevates a slave:

In spite of the well known fact of being slave before being guided to Islam, after becoming a Muslim Bilal Habashi ؓ became, in time, the head *muaddhin* of the Noble Prophet ﷺ, making him, as it were, the patron saint of all *muaddhins* to come thereafter. The most vivid evidence for this is the *Ya Hadrat Bilai Habashi* panels, in most exquisite calligraphy, adorning the inner walls of mosques across Muslim lands.

Similarly, after being granted freedom by the Prophet of Mercy ﷺ, to whom he was presented as a gift by the honorable Khadijah ﷺ, Zayd ibn Harithah ﷺ, that gracious Companion, lived a life imbued with bounteous love for the Prophet, cherished as a supreme example for countless virtues. At a very tender age, his son Usamah ﷺ was personally appointed by the Noble Messenger ﷺ as the commander-in-chief of the Muslim army.

One may also recall Tariq ibn Ziyad, the captor of Spain, previously an enchained slave bought and sold at will. Thanks to Islam, however, he was elevated to a rank worthy of the dignity and honor of man, ending up becoming the commander of the Muslim army.

Islam, in short, turned slaves into masters. Such was, after all, the main motive for the staunch idolater opposition of Islam in the first place. Now, do not contemporary doubters, the disbelievers of the 21st century carry the exact features? Do not the tyrants of today consign many free people to a life no different than slavery? Under the pretext of bringing liberty, are not the rights of countless innocent and helpless communities impounded for the sole reason of exploitation? Is there really that much difference, one wonders, between the oppressions of the past and the modern system of slavery atrociously implemented throughout the world as we speak, under the garb of a likable schema of terms and concepts?

Thus, in this day and age, Islam's appreciation of human value, the force behind the gradual abolishment of slavery, by virtue of introducing ameliorating principles and responsibilities, ought to be recognized as the remedy of humanity. Otherwise it is set to perish in the bloody and brutal claws of exploitative notions that, under the promise of freedom, bring nothing but captivity. A far cry are the corrupt, leechlike principles that, when looking at the weak souls on earth, see nothing but flesh to be blood-sucked, to be shackled into slavery, from the sublimity of Islam that has used every given opportunity to put into place protecting measures to the advantage of both captives and servants, epitomized in the words of the Great Prophet ﷺ:

"*They are your brothers and sisters...clothe and feed them in the same way you would yourselves.*"[34]

Like yesterday and so today, obeying the Prophet of Grace ﷺ therefore stands as the sole cure for mankind; insofar as it was him who made sure that each human being, irrespective of whether rich or poor, strong or weak, lived worthy of the title, and brought unshakable measures in ensuring mankind received the honor it merits. Such that when some Companions asked the Prophet ﷺ the amount of times they ought to forgive their servants, he recommended them to:

"*Forgive them seventy times a day, every day.*" (Abu Dawud, Adab, 123-124/5164; Tirmidhi, Birr, 31/1949)

The advice below of the Gracious Prophet ﷺ, an unfathomable ocean of mercy, exposes an inexpressible level considerateness for the other:

"*When your servants bring food to your table, even if you are not going to have them sit with you, at least offer them some of the food...for it was them that endured the heat and struggle of cooking.*" (Bukhari, Atimah, 55; Tirmidhi, Atimah, 44)

34. Muslim, Aymân, 36-38.

Had Allah, glory unto Him, willed, He could have turned things upon their heels, making the servant the master and the master the servant. It is our duty therefore to thank Allah and treat those in our care with in the best possible way.

The Prophet of Allah's ﷺ Treatment of Women

Women, in the Age of Ignorance, were exacted with an ignominious conduct, detrimental to female honor. From fear that they may fall into prostitution, people would ruthlessly bury their female children alive. Actuated by hearts of stone, they were committing a greater crime to prevent another, essentially caused by none other than ignorance. Their conditions are lucidly depicted by the Almighty in the Quran:

"**And when a daughter is announced to one of them his face becomes black and he is full of wrath.**" (an-Nahl, 58)

Seen solely as means for pleasure, women were treated humiliatingly. But with the command of the Blessed Prophet ﷺ women's rights were established, enabling women to become examples of integrity and virtue in society. Motherhood became an expression of honor.

The Prophetic praise articulated in the hadith, "*Paradise lies under the feet of mothers*",[35] symbolizes the value women have deservedly attained.

The Noble Prophet's ﷺ courtesy towards women is wonderfully illustrated in the incident below:

35. Nasâî, Jihâd, 6; Ahmad, III, 429; Suyutî, I, 125.

Once during a journey, a servant by the name of Anjasha began chanting to speed up the camels.[36] Concerned that the accelerated camels might harm the delicate bodies of the women riding them, the Prophet of Grace ﷺ remarked, allusively:

"*Be cautious, Anjasha, so that you don't shatter the glasses!*" (Bukhari, Adab, 95; Ahmad, III, 117)

The Prophet ﷺ has stated, in another hadith:

"*Allah…I urgently avoid others from violating the rights of the two weak: orphans and women.*" (Ibn Majah, Adab, 6)

"*A Muslim ought not to hate his wife…for if she has a habit he dislikes, there will be another he likes.*" (Muslim, Rada, 61)

Women are not bushes of thorn that deserve aversion, but rather rosaries that merit love and affection; and these are sentiments granted none other than by the Almighty. One can recall, in relation, the below words of the Prophet ﷺ:

"*I have been made to like, from your world, women and fragrance…and salat has been rendered the spark of my eyes.*" (Nasai, Ishratu'n-Nisa, 10; Ahmad, III, 128, 199)

That women, through whom human beings are delivered into the world, have been rendered lovable to the Prophet ﷺ should not be assessed with from a perspective of ignorance.[37]

---

36. Camels are infatuated by a chant and a nice voice, hence the chanting of shepherds, called *hida*, to get their camels moving.
37. Finding even a glimpse of an inclination of personal desire in any of the contracted marriages of the Blessed Prophet ﷺ is impossible. Having never proposed to a girl even during in his youth, the Prophet ﷺ accepted the proposal of the honorable Khadijah, a forty year old widow with children, with whom he spent the most vigorous years of his life. His marriages thereafter correspond to

It should be borne in mind that this love, placed within the natural disposition of man by Allah, is a step of affection on a ladder that leads to a greater kind of love. What is of virtue, therefore, is not a contemptible kind of obsession towards women, much rather it is to give them the sublime value they deserve. In the history of humankind, it has only been within the blissful clime of Islam that women have attained such a divine worth. All other systems that allegedly cherish women cherish them only as fleshes for display, meanwhile economically exploiting them behind the scenes, manipulating them for their depraved ends.

The perspective toward women today, therefore, must be reassessed upon propitious and sublime base of Islam and thereby reinstalled in its proper zone. Woman and man are two profound worlds that have complemented one another since the beginning of their creation. But in this complementing process, Allah, glory unto Him, has bestowed a more influential role upon women; such that they can either make or break societies. Thus Islam has embraced, as a paramount

---

his more elderly years, post fifty-four to be precise; none of which were contracted, again, out of personal desire, but through Divine behest, and all of which were underlain with propitious reasons, first and foremost being the educating of Muslim women. Furthermore, the noble women fortunate to be wed to the Prophet ﷺ were mostly helpless and elderly women with children from previous marriages. Thus the conspicuous fact that the polygamous phase of the Blessed Prophet ﷺ coincides with his mature years and moreover at a time in which the duty of prophethood was at its most hectic, clearly proves that the marriages were Divinely orchestrated, actuated with the aim of conveying Islam to masses with greater ease. For more detailed information see, Osman Nûri Topbaş, *Hazret-i Muhammed Mustafâ,* I, 130-140.

ideal, the upbringing of women destined to be makers, as made actual by the words of the Noble Prophet ﷺ below:

"*Whoever takes under his wings his three daughters or sisters, beautifully rears and educates them, gets them married and continues his blessings and aids towards them, is destined for Paradise.*" (Abu Dawud, Adab, 120-121/5147; Tirmidhi, Birr, 13/1912; Ahmad, III, 97)

The Noble Prophet ﷺ has stated in another similar hadith:

"*Whosoever sees the rearing and educating of his two daughters to their maturity, on the Day of Judgment he and I shall be by each other's side like this*", joining his two fingers together in illustration. (Muslim, Birr, 149; Tirmidhi, Birr, 13/1914)

And in emphasis of the value of a pious woman, he said:

"*Earth is but a fleeting benefit…and the most beneficial of its inhabitants is a righteous, pious woman.*" (Muslim, Rada, 64; Nasai, Nikah, 15; Ibn Majah, Nikah, 5)

Standing strong behind great men, more often than not, are virtuous women. Amid the tough times of the first call, for instance, the Noble Messenger ﷺ found his first and most resilient support in the honorable Khadijah, something the Prophet ﷺ dearly appreciated till the end of his life. Evident also is the role of the great Fatimah in the successes of Ali ؓ.

A pious woman is thus the greatest and most valuable asset the earth can offer, wherefore the Prophet ﷺ has placed emphasis on treating them with care as a prerequisite of becoming virtuous, in the following words:

"*The most perfect Believer is he with the most excellent morals; and the most virtuous of you is he who treats women with the greatest integrity.*" (Tirmidhi, Rada, 11/1162)

Yet what a slump of depravity it must be to still identify women only as a means for pleasure, to see them as possessions to relieve the desires of the flesh and to focus only on their physical characteristics. It betrays an ignorance of the matter, blindness to the magnificent features granted to women by the Almighty. The fact that women have been exposed in the consumer society today and exploited as a tool for advertisement is a major and destructive blow to the pride and integrity of women.

In fact women ought to be raised as the true architects of society, a heavenly lap rearing the intellects of tomorrow. There has not been created any other being worthy of the love and respect truly deserved by such genuine mothers, who have carried us for a while in their bellies, then in their arms and then till death in their hearts. A loyal mother to have sacrificed her own for her family warrants a profound love, a vast respect and a lifelong gratitude.

As for fragrance, the underlying wisdom for it being rendered lovable to the Blessed Prophet ﷺ lies in the deepness and sensitivity it grants the soul. A beautiful scent is a sweet breeze of bliss also enjoyed by angels. It is moreover a mark of cleanliness, for a clean person naturally smells nice. The tender skin of the Blessed Prophet ﷺ in fact always smelt as if it had been scented in the fragrance of roses; better still it was like roses had been created in the first place from the sweat trickling forth from his body. Whenever he caressed a child's head, the head of the child would for a long while smell of musk.

With respect to salat, it was made the light of the Prophet's ﷺ eyes, since salat is a meeting with Allah, glory unto Him, a deed of worship performed like the Almighty is present before the person; and as such, it is the spark of the eye.

The Prophet of Allah's ﷺ Treatment of Orphans

That Allah, glory unto Him, sent His Beloved as an orphan to the world has granted orphanage an especial value. The Blessed Prophet ﷺ would show enormous concern for the caring of orphans, the protection of whom is enjoined on numerous occasions throughout the Quran.

Commanding the espousal of sensitivity towards orphans, the Almighty states:

"**…Therefore, treat not the orphan with harshness.**" (ad-Duha, 9)

The related hadiths are of a similar tone:

"*The house of greatest benefit for Muslims is that in which an orphan is treated with compassion…and the worst is that in which an orphan is treated with cruelty.*" (Ibn Majah, Adab, 6)

"*If a person takes an orphan, from among Muslims, home to feed and to clothe, then unless he commits an unforgivable sin, Allah, glory unto Him, will surely put him in Paradise.*" (Tirmidhi, Birr, 14/1917)

"If a person caresses the head of an orphan simply for the sake of Allah, he will receive a reward for every strand of hair his hand touches..." (Ahmad, V, 250)

The Messenger of Allah ﷺ would persistently recommend the fulfilling of required social responsibilities in nursing the brokenhearted of society.

"Whoever treats well an orphan under his care, he and I shall be together in Paradise," he would say, joining his fingers together to indicate the closeness of their awaiting company. (Bukhari, Adab, 24)

Once, to one complaining about the hardness of his heart, the Prophet of Mercy ﷺ advised:

"Feed a poor, caress the head of an orphan, if you want to soften your heart." (Ahmad, II, 263, 387)

The Prophet ﷺ, the peak of mercy and compassion, has again asserted:

"I am closer to Believers than they are to themselves. If a person bequeaths wealth following his death, then his inheritors shall lay claim to it. But if he leaves behind personal debt or orphans, then his debt is mine to close, and his orphans are mine to take care of." (Muslim, Juma, 43. See also, Ibn Majah, Muqaddimah, 7)

The Prophet of Allah's ﷺ Treatment of Animals

Every behavior of the Prophet of Mercy ﷺ was founded upon the pedestal of love and compassion, stemming from approaching all creatures with a feeling of love and a desire toward attending to their needs. Receiving a share of this vast ocean of compassion was also the animal kingdom. The Age of Ignorance was notorious, among many other reasons, for its unspeakable cruelty towards animals; they would severe bits of animals to eat while they were still alive and organize unrestrained fighting contests between animals. The Noble Prophet ﷺ put an end to such atrocious practices.

The below account is by Abu Waqid ﷺ:

"Medinans used to slice the lump of camels and likewise sever the legs of sheep to consume while the animals were still alive. The Messenger of Allah ﷺ intervened, declaring, '*whatever is severed from an alive animal is carcass and therefore inedible.*'" (Tirmidhi, Sayd, 12/1480)

The Prophet ﷺ once, while walking, saw a donkey whose face had been branded. Disturbed, he remarked:

"*May the wrath of Allah follow the responsible!*" (Bukhari, Zhabaih, 25)

A group, that caused a bird distress by stealing one of her hatchlings from her nest, became the recipients of the admonishing of the Noble Prophet ﷺ:

"*Whoever took the hatchling of the poor bird, return it to her at once!*" he commanded. (Abu Dawud, Adab, 163-164/5268)

Accompanied by his Companions, the Messenger of Allah ﷺ had once set out from Medina to Mecca, in *ihram*. Near Usayah, he saw a fawn curled up, sleeping under a shade. The Blessed Prophet ﷺ then commanded one of the Companions present to watch over the fawn and ensure nobody did anything to frighten the animal. (Muwatta, Hajj; Nasai, Hajj, 78)

Again, leading his magnificent army of ten-thousand strong to seize Mecca, the Prophet of Grace ﷺ on the way stumbled upon a dog, sprawled out breastfeeding her puppies. He quickly called Juayl ibn Suraqa and commanded him to stand guard over the dogs, instructing the army to refrain from doing anything that may cause the mother and her pups distress. (Waqidi, II, 804)

Seeing a camel once, skeletal from being undernourished, the Prophet ﷺ commented:

"*Fear the Almighty with regard to these animals that cannot speak. Ride and feed on them as they are fit.*" (Abu Dawud, Jihad, 44/2548)

Having once entered a garden belonging to an Ansari man, the Blessed Prophet ﷺ there saw a camel, which seeing the Prophet ﷺ began bellowing with tears trickling forth from its eyes. The Noble Messenger ﷺ went next to the camel and gently began caressing behind its ears, only after which the camel calmed down.

"*Who owns this camel?*" the Prophet ﷺ thereupon asked.

"It is mine", said an approaching young Medinan man.

"*Don't you fear Allah with regard to the animal He has blessed you with?*" asked the Prophet ﷺ. "*It complains to me that you have left it in hunger and overworked it.*" (Abu Dawud, Jihad, 44/2549)

On yet another occasion, while walking, the Messenger of Allah ﷺ encountered a group of people, chatting to each other while astride on their animal. He advised them to:

"*...ride your animals with care, without tiring them and rest them appropriately while you are not using them. Do not use them as seats to accommodate the conversations you have* *on the streets. Many a ridden animal is better than its rider and remembers Allah, the Glorious, more than him."* (Ahmad, III, 439)

The Blessed Prophet ﷺ, during another time, came across a man slaughtering a sheep. The man, after having placed the sheep on the ground, began to sharpen his knife right before its eyes, an insensitive act incurring the warning of the Blessed Prophet ﷺ:

"*Do you wish to kill the animal more than once? Couldn't you have sharpened your knife before you had laid the sheep on the ground?*" (Hakim, IV, 257, 260)

"*Should I tell you about those who are distant from Hellfire and from whom Hellfire is equally distant?*" he once asked to his Companions, before going on to give the answer:

"*The courteous, tenderhearted, compassionate, friendly and affectionate...*" (Ahmad, I, 415)

The Blessed Prophet ﷺ explicates the contrast between the compassionate and the cruel in the subsequent depiction:

"*A sinful woman once saw a dog, in a desert, licking the sand from thirst. Feeling sorry for it, she used her shoe to draw water from a nearby well and thereby quenched the dog's thirst. So Allah forgave her sins. Another woman, careless, left her cat to starve; she prevented the cat from even helping itself to crawling bugs to allay its hunger. The cat finally died of starvation, and the woman's cruelty earned her a place in Hell.*"[38]

Through these measures, the Blessed Prophet ﷺ effectively turned a society of ignorance into a generation worthy

38. See, Bukhârî, Anbiyâ, 54; Muslim, Salâm, 151, 154; Birr, 133; Nasâî, Kusûf, 14.

of the Age of Bliss, *Asr'us-Saadah*. People, once grievously dreadful even in their treatment of each other, were now filled with a mercy that extended even to animals, for the very reason that the Prophet ﷺ, their exemplar beyond compare, was observing the rights of creatures as little as sparrows and immersing his Companions in an ineffable sensitivity.

Even with harmful animals like snakes and scorpions, needed at times to be killed for self defense, the Prophet ﷺ sympathetically commands their killing, if need be, in the least hurtful manner:

"*Whoever kills a snake in one go will receive a hundred rewards. Less for he who has two goes, and lesser for he who has more.*" (Muslim, Salam 147; Abu Dawud, Adab 162-163/5263, Sayd, 14/1482)

How profound a compassion it must be where it is extends to even the killing of dangerous animals…

❁

The Noble Prophet ﷺ never boasted of possessing such a lofty standard of morals and servanthood. He would sometimes enumerate the blessings given to him by the Almighty, complementing it however with the assuring words, "*La Fakhra - no boasting*", enshrouding himself in humbleness beyond description. (Tirmidhi, Manaqib, 1; Ibn Majah, Zuhd, 37; Ahmad, I, 5, 281)

Pride, or boasting, aims toward attracting praise and admiration, which fuel the arrogance of human beings. In spite of being the noblest of mankind and being of object of Divine accolades, the Blessed Prophet ﷺ would always tell his Companions to call him:

"*...the servant and the messenger of Allah*" (Bukhari, Anbiya, 48; Ahmad, I, 23)

Human beings are endowed with the feeling of servanthood. One either serves his possessions and ends that are to his advantage, or his Lord. Servanthood to the Lord protects one from slavery to the self and possessions.

The perfect balance instituted by the Noble Messenger ﷺ between the opposites of life exposes not the slightest deficiency or shortcoming. Discerning a second example of such character throughout history is impossible.

In particular walks of life, it is possible to perceive heroes with superior skills and qualities. But the Prophet ﷺ stands strong as the sole example of the furthermost instances of all qualities combined in one person. Succinctly stated, he is most exceptional personality of all time, in all aspects thinkable, who left a legacy of unmatched beauties for the entire humankind, material and spiritual; unfathomable virtues in servanthood, social interactions and morals.

For no other reason, than that he was a guide of eternal bliss, deeply conscious of the heavy responsibility of being an exemplar for his *ummah*...

In close relation, the Blessed Prophet's ﷺ sensitivity towards salat was beyond everything else. Only a little time of night would he reserve for sleeping, while keeping his blessed body from the comfort of the bed for the better part of it. While everyone slept amid their sweet dreams, he would be shedding tears, prostrating to the Almighty. Even during his final days when his illness began taking its toll, the Noble Prophet ﷺ observed congregational salat as much as his strength allowed him to step out of his room into the Masjid.

Abdullah ibn Shikhkir ﷺ depicts the Prophet's ﷺ focus during salat as follows:

"I once went next to the Messenger of Allah ﷺ. He was performing salat, and from the intensity of his crying there were sounds similar to a boiling cauldron coming from his chest like." (Abu Dawud, Salat, 156-157/904; Nasai, Sahv, 18)

Even though there was not any compulsory fasting for Muslims other than that of Ramadan, it was very rare for there to be a month in which the Gracious Prophet ﷺ would not be seen fasting.

The honorable Aisha ﷺ says:

"The Messenger of Allah ﷺ would at times fast so continuously that we would think he was never going to stop." (Bukhari, Sawm, 53)

He would never neglect fasting during the thirteenth, fourteenth and fifteenth days of each month, six days during Shawwal and the *ashura* fasting on the tenth of Muharram. In addition, it was habitual for him to fast on Mondays and Thursdays.

Though he would enjoin the Believers, through the verse of zakah, with almsgiving and donating charity, the Noble Messenger ﷺ would always provide the greatest amount of charities himself. He had set the highest standard of breathing life into the Divine praise:

"**...who believe in the Unseen, are steadfast in prayer, and spend out of what We have provided for them**" (al-Baqara, 3). He always praised possessions spared for charity, along with traders who upheld piety.

Standards from the Stars

A characteristic unique to him, the Noble Prophet ﷺ would never store anything worldly, donating instead whatever he had in his hands on the way of Allah, glory unto Him. Abu Zharr ؓ recounts:

"We were walking with the Messenger of Allah ﷺ in outer Medina on a rocky field. Mount Uhud appeared from a distance.

'*Abu Zharr*!' said the Messenger of Allah ﷺ.

'Yes', replied I.

'*Having gold as much as Mount Uhud would not make me happy*', he said. '*Except for that which I would keep aside to close a debt, I would not wish to set aside even a dime for more than three days*.'" (Muslim, Zakat, 32; Bukhari, Istiqrad, 3)

There would be times when he would fast two, maybe three days on end without break, cautioning the Companions wanting to follow in his footsteps, saying:

"*You can not endure it*," banning them trying to do the same. (Bukhari, Sawm, 48)

We must therefore touch upon the fact that as important as it is to know that the Noble Messenger ﷺ is, for us, the sole guide and exemplar, it is of equal importance to be aware of the standards of emulating him, insofar as his behavior and acts fall under two categories, namely:

1. Those that bind him only;

2. Those that bind all.

Consequently, we are not obliged to follow his example in virtues that are peculiar to the Prophet's ﷺ sublime character; for deeds of such profound virtue are virtually standards from the stars, which we do not have the power to perform. But with respect to acts and behavior that come under the second category, we stand compelled to emulate the Prophet ﷺ and follow in his dazzling footsteps as much as it is allowed by our power and competence, until the very end of our lives.

Although attaining to the Prophet's ﷺ level of individual perfection remains a sheer impossibility, still, each person devoted to following his lead can become a little 'Muhammad' in his own world. That the Turks have dub their soldiers defending the frontiers of Muslim lands 'Mehmetçik' i.e. Little Muhammad, is inspired by this delicate consideration.

To elaborate, insofar as compulsory deeds like almsgiving are financially assessed, we are in a position to know the amount to give that would relieve us of the relevant responsibility. But it is impossible for us to know in exactitude our degree of responsibility for all the other opportunities and abilities we have been blessed with by the Almighty, for which reason we are compelled to live a life of servanthood till we breathe our last.

The sturdiest scales on which we can weigh our positions are provided by the *Ansar* and *Muhajirun*, the Companions reared under the spiritual training of the Prophet of Grace ﷺ; the Companions who, in order to pay the price for the blessings they were endowed with, traveled to lands as far as Central Asia and China to convey the Call, never showing even a glimpse of tiredness in their *iman* enthused struggle.

Part Three

- The Heart's Blend in Following the Prophet of Allah ﷺ
- Adhering to the Prophet of Allah ﷺ with Love
- The Mirror of His Love and Morals: *Asr'us-Saadah*
- Touching Hymns of Prophetic Love
- *Salawat'us-Sharifah*

The Heart's Blend in Following the Prophet of Allah ﷺ

Appropriately benefiting from the quintessential example of the Blessed Prophet ﷺ and thereby acquiring a nearness to the excellent morals of the Companions, requires, first of all, the attainment of a blend of the heart. The relevant *ayah* speaks loud and clear:

"Certainly you have in the Messenger of Allah an *uswat'ul-hasanah* –a quintessential example- for him who hopes in Allah and the Hereafter and remembers Allah much." (al-Ahzab, 21)

As can be seen, 'hoping in Allah and the Hereafter' and 'remembering Allah much', constitute the imperative steps in receiving an appropriate share of the exemplary character of the Prophet ﷺ.

Unlike deeds of worship which are fulfilled during certain times, the safeguarding of belief in the Almighty is something that is required constantly. Each moment is a time to pay the price for believing in Allah, glory unto Him, and seeking His pleasure. Being in the state of *dhikr'ud-daim*, a constant remembrance, is therefore of necessity, to shield the heart from falling weak, to reinforce its resistance against Satanic and self oriented whispers and, most of all, to ensure there is not a moment in which the Almighty is forgotten.

The Almighty commands, throughout numerous verses:

"*O Believers! Remember Allah with much remembrance*!"[39] But because verses of the kind do not set a limit on the required number of remembrances, the command of *dhikr*, remembrance, is to be understood as alluding to the greatest amount possible.[40] Required of the Believer therefore is to remember Allah at all times and places possible, to the utmost of capacity.

Stated in another verse:

"**And those who disbelieve say: Why is not a sign sent down upon him by his Lord? Say: Surely Allah makes him who will go astray, and guides to Himself those who turn to Him. Those who believe and whose hearts are set at rest by the remembrance of Allah; now surely by Allah's remembrance are the hearts set at rest.**" (ar-Rad, 27-28)

Remembering Allah, without a doubt, is not simply the literal repetition of the name 'Allah', much rather it is to facilitate the Divine Name in the heart, the focal point of the capacity to feel, to let it find its place therein, and infuse the heart thereby with its serenity and zest. Engrossing the heart in Divine remembrance rids it of all its maladies, purifies its ingrained dirt and rust for light to enter; and then having been refined to sensitivity, it becomes all set for Divine mysteries. When each heart beat is attuned to the Truth, intentions and deeds are uplifted to greater worth.

39. al-Ahzab, 41; Also see, al-Jum'a, 10
40. Given that a certain quantitative command is not followed by a further clarification to spell out its limit, then, as a rule, the command is taken to imply the utmost or most virtuous amount possible.

The Messenger of Allah ﷺ professes:

"*The sign of loving Allah is to love His remembrance.*" (Suyuti, II, 52)

Lovers never cease thinking of their beloved; forever talking about them, never letting them slip out of their hearts. Indeed, souls bent on living the delightful life of *iman* perpetuate Divine remembrance deep within their hearts. Standing, sitting or laying on their sides, they plunge into deep contemplation about the delicate and subtle wisdom behind the creation the skies and the Earth, and remark, in awe:

"**Our Lord...You have not created this in vain! Glory be to You; save us then from the punishment of the fire!**" (Ali Imran, 191)

Allah wants little to do with a heart that has not acquired such depth and elegance, as attested by the below *ayah*:

"**...then woe unto those whose hearts are hardened against remembrance of Allah.**" (Zumar, 22)

Standing aloof from *dhikr*, as indicated by the verse, is tantamount to a loss of human integrity.

Thus in a word, adherence to the Blessed Prophet and aptly benefiting from him demands hearts be filled with Divine Love, and by virtue of slipping away from mortal desires, be adorned with the remembrance of Allah, coupled with the yearning to meet Him and the Hereafter.

Adhering to the Prophet of Allah ﷺ with Love

The natural result of a true love felt for the Prophet of Grace ﷺ is an unconditional devotion to his path and a sincere compliance with and submission to him.

Such a personality the Blessed Prophet ﷺ is that, in all aspects, he is pure mercy for mankind. Wonderfully exhibiting the profound degree of the mercy and compassion embedded in his heart, for Believers, is the following verse:

"Certainly a Messenger has come to you from among yourselves; grievous to him is your falling into distress, excessively solicitous respecting you; to the believers (he is) compassionate." (at-Tawba, 128)

A hadith illustrating the immense compassion he had for his *ummah* runs as follows:

"Believers...! May Allah keep you safe! May He watch over you...protect you from harm and help You! May He exalt you... and guide you through! May He take you into His protection! May He keep you removed from all kinds of adversities and protect your religion for you!"[41]

41. Tabaranî, Awsat, IV, 208; Abû Nuaym, *Hilyatu'l-Awliyâ*, Beirut 1967, IV, 168.

A guiding light, the Blessed Prophet ﷺ was an epitome of mercy that through the words, behavior and a life of integrity manifesting therefrom, encompassed the entire humankind. On the way to guiding others, he was burdened under the greatest of hardships. So great was his passion and zeal for the guidance of his *ummah* and for ensuring they were all granted Divine amnesty, the Prophet would sometimes receive a Divine caution not to devastate himself:

"Then maybe you will kill yourself with grief, sorrowing after them, if they do not believe in this call!" (al-Kahf, 6)

"Perhaps you will kill yourself with grief because they do not believe!" (as-Shuara, 3)

The verses are proof that springing from his extreme compassion, the Noble Prophet ﷺ genuinely wished for all people on Earth to believe in the Almighty and thereby save themselves from the torment of Hell.

Now it is on us to ponder our own adequacy in responding to the immense benevolence and love nurtured by the Prophet of Mercy ﷺ for his *ummah*.

Depending on how we espouse the Prophet's ﷺ *hal* (spiritual states) under the guidance of the Quran and, again, in accordance with the behavior of the Prophet ﷺ, the degree of our love for him will undeniably surface. How did the Companions, who loved him and sacrificed their all in his way, really feel the Prophet ﷺ? How did they become one with his conduct and reflect his morals onto their lives? And where exactly do we stand in all this? Our love for the Prophet ﷺ must stand the test of this scale, a gateway to embellish our hearts with his morals. All our sins and shortcomings, and above all our inner revolts must be rinsed in the pure stream of his morals, an ocean of meaning and wisdom, wherefrom we must seek the sprinkle of life for a spiritual revival.

The secret of *wasl ila'Allah*, reaching Allah, glory unto Him, lies in getting closer, with an untainted heart, to the Quran, the word of the Almighty, and the Sunnah of the Prophet ﷺ, as well as loving what is loved by Allah and His Prophet and despising what is duly despised by them.

Attuning affections towards what is loved by the Divine keeps the heart alive and spirited, steering it to goodness. Love and its opposite hate never come together in a single heart; though most certainly, as the heart cannot bare a void, the absence of one is the reason of existence for the other. The difference between the opposites is as infinite as the distance between the *ala'ul-illiyyin*, the highest of the high, and *asfal'us-safilin*, the lowest of the low.

Poet Kemâl Edib Kürkçüoğlu, evocatively instructs and at once warns Believers neglectful of the love and the Sunnah of the Messenger of Allah ﷺ:

To be thrown distant from his attention,
In both lives suffices for the neglectful as ruin...

May our Lord render us an *ummah* devoted to him with love...

Whilst being savagely pelted with stones by the very people whose guidance the Prophet ﷺ was striving towards, and still benevolently praying for their wellbeing, with the astonished Zayd ibn Harithah remarking in the background:

"You still pray for them, Messenger of Allah, while they put you through the heaviest of ordeals?", he was still able to say:

"*What else can I do...I was sent as mercy not as cruelty!*" Does not that alone testify to the unreachable level of his kindness and compassion?

With the long awaited prophethood of the Noble Messenger ﷺ humankind was united with the most perfect of its guiding lights. Therefore, those crammed in their egotistic lives in the present day, in effect stand under a greater responsibility than those who were indulging in lives of ignorance before the arrival of such an exemplary guide.

In our times, marked by an enchantment with power, by which mankind, already under the spell of the ego, is charmed, we remain in an even more desperate need to construct our characters in alignment with that of the Light of Being ﷺ. Doubtless, the greatest influence during the glory days of our history was the existence of Believers, people of virtuous deeds who were the true inheritors of that Great Prophet ﷺ, and their presenting to society, in the flesh, their exemplary characters. In contrast, we are lamentably made to witness one of the most unfortunate realities of today as being a decadence of spirituality, due to an insufficient number of such exemplary figures.

In order, to once again, get in touch with the exhilarating inner levels of the Blessed Prophet ﷺ and those who have striven in his path, and above all, the heroes of the heart so abundant throughout our history, it is imperative we have access to monumental and exemplary figures of the kind mentioned.

For that, it is required we hear them, understand their ways and thus obtain a share of their rich inner worlds; that is to say, how they conceived this passing life and opened up the way of happiness, for both themselves and the entire humankind, by the manner in which they used their intellect, their lives and the means granted to them by Allah, glory unto Him.

The Mirror of His Love and Morals: *Asr'us-Saadah*

Such an inspiring elixir were the outer manners imparted by the Blessed Prophet ﷺ and the internal influence he exerted, that in rapid time they lifted an ignorant society previously in the wilderness, most of whom were ignorant of even the basics of being human, to a level undreamed of, as 'the Companions', who still remain an object of the envy of mankind even today. They were united under one religion, the same flag, law and culture, under the banner of a mutual government and civilization.

The Noble Prophet ﷺ educated the brute and the brutal, rendered the wild civilized and turned the base into pillars of piety and righteousness, spilling over with the love and fear of the Almighty.

A ignorant society, unable for centuries on end to raise a single person worthy of significance, thanks to the enriching spirituality of the Blessed Prophet ﷺ, suddenly began rearing numerous figures of preeminence, who, like flames of knowledge and wisdom, carried the inspiration within their hearts over to the four corners of the world. Taking eternity under its shade, the Light that descended on the desert instilled truth, justice and guidance to entire humanity. The *law'laka law'laka*[42] mystery became manifest, and the reason for the creation of the universe was fulfilled.

The people of the *Asr'us-Saadah*, the Age of Bliss, raised under the supervision of the Noble Prophet ﷺ, the greatest example mankind could ever dream to have, were a society of *marifa*, of true wisdom. The period was that of deep contemplation, a time to gain closer acquaintance with The Almighty and His Messenger. Placing *tawhid* in the center of their thought and ideal, the Companions were triumphant in ridding their hearts of worldly gains, the idols within. Lives and possessions were relegated to the position of means. The zest of *iman* was tasted. Mercy grew deeper. Service to the cause became a lifestyle. A sacrifice unthinkable was put on display, crystallized in the quintessential Islamic character. Just to hear a celebrated word of the Blessed Prophet ﷺ, a Companion would walk a month's distance, only to return without hearing; all but witnessing the person tricking his horse enough to question his veracity.

So what did the Companions obtain from the Blessed Prophet ﷺ?

Iniqas, a reflection, mirroring of the Prophet ﷺ, becoming one with him.

Acquirement of *aqrabiyyah*; nearness to Allah, glory unto Him, and recognizing Him in the heart.

Thus the good and the right became manifest with all their beauty in their hearts, and the evil and wrong became visible with all its ugliness.

42. "Had you not been, had you not been, (I would not have created the universe)." For the relevant hadith see, Hâkim, II, 672/4228.

The Companions developed a new understanding of the Almighty, the universe and the self. Their aim became to become one with the entire *hal* of the Prophet of Grace ﷺ, akin to how the sun reflects on to a small mirror.

The borders of the small Muslim city-state founded in Medina, comprised approximately of four-hundred families, reached Iraq and Palestine, only in a matter of ten years. The Companions were at war with Byzantine and Persia at the time of the bereavement of the Noble Messenger ﷺ, though their standards of living had little changed as compared to ten years before. They continued persisting in their lives of abstinence. Excess consumption, greed, luxury and pomp were things unknown to the Companions, imbued with a constant awareness that 'awaiting the flesh, tomorrow, was but the grave.' They therefore always fled the tendency of reserving the pleasures of the world to themselves and indulging too much in them. With the excitement and zest of *iman*, they instead used them as means for guiding humankind to its salvation. They molded their lives in the cast of seeking the pleasure of Allah, glory unto Him.

Without a doubt one of the most prominent reasons for the clear and rapid spread of Islam, like a glaring flash of morning light, among the oppressed and the exploited, was the fact that the Companions showed a perfect Muslim character wherever they stepped foot. The elite students of the Blessed Prophet ﷺ, the Companions were Believers par excellence, honest and just, carrying treasures of benevolence in their hearts enlightened by the Prophetic light, who looked upon fellow servants of the Almighty only with eyes of compassion.

In the hub of friendship, they had placed Allah, glory unto Him, and His Messenger, which elevated them, an illiterate society, to the peak of civilization. Their hearts were perpetually excited, thinking 'What would Allah want from us?' or 'How would the Messenger of Allah like to see us?'

Centuries were shaped by them, stemming from an age of bliss granted to humankind.

Freed from the evil of the *nafs'ul-ammara*, 'the evil commanding self', they became Believers who constantly questioned themselves, raised above their wildness to an angelic character.

Qarafi (d.684 AH), one of the most important figures in the methodology of Islamic law, states:

"Had there not been another miracle of our Noble Messenger ﷺ, the righteous Companions he raised would have been sufficient to prove his prophethood."

They were the miracle of the Quran come to life; peaks of human virtue excelling in prudence, competence and all humanitarian values.

In that age, both reason and heart, means which attain Believers perfection, were mutually put to use, in a graceful harmony. By keeping the elements of excitement of love alive, thinking was pushed deeper. People lived with the consciousness of the world being a school of trials. Hearts became familiar with the flows of Divine Power. Journeys to lands as far as Samarkand and China, for the sake of enjoining the good and prohibiting the evil, became commonplace, with those to follow carrying the flame further to Andalusia. That society of ignorance developed into people with *real* knowledge'.

Nights became day, winters spring. Contemplation developed, becoming a profound peer into how the human body came to be from a drop of liquid, birds from simple eggs, trees and fruits from insignificant seeds, and alike wonders. The direction of human life took a turn towards the pleasure of the Creator. Feelings of mercy and compassion, the deepness of spreading the truth acquired a vastness previously unseen.

Moments in which the message of *tawhid* was communicated became, for the Companions, the sweetest and most meaningful times of life. An illustrious Companion once thanked a wretched man who allowed three minutes before hanging him, saying:

"...that means I have another three minutes to enjoin the good."

In a nutshell, the Companions lived with and for the Quran, devoting their lives to the Sacred Book, displaying a sacrifice and perseverance never before witnessed throughout history. Inflicted with torture and oppression, subjected to cruelty, still, they never compromised an inch of what they believed. To bring to life the verses sent forth by the Almighty, they migrated, leaving behind all their homes and belongings, proving they knew what sacrifice meant, in the truest sense of the word.

They always aspired to learn and live each *ayah* appropriately, never straying from the Quran even in times most dangerous. Abbad ﷺ, designated by the Prophet ﷺ as watchman, informed his fellow guard Ammar ﷺ of an attack only after having been on the receiving end of two or three arrows. To Ammar, somewhat taken aback, asking him as to why he did not inform him after the first arrow, Abbad ﷺ replied:

"I was reciting a *surah* of the Quran and I did not want to break my *salat* before having completed its recital. But when the arrows hit me one after another I stopped reciting and bowed to *ruqu*. But by Allah, had there not been a fear of losing this spot whose protection the Messenger of Allah ordered, I would have preferred death over cutting my recital of the chapter short." (Abu Dawud, Taharat, 78/198; Ahmad, III, 344; Ibn Hisham, III, 219; Waqidi, I, 397)

The Companions led a life that revolved around the Quran. Each religious obligation, for them, was an insatiable taste. Each verse revealed was like a feast from heaven. All efforts were channeled to properly understand the Quran and to bring it to life in the most exemplary fashion. What a magnificent portrait of virtue it must have been that a female Companion saw sufficient dowry in asking the groom to simply teach her parts of the Quran he knew.[43]

They preferred waking during the night to perform salat, to recite at daybreak their prayers and reciting the Quran over their warm beds. Passers by in the dark of the night would hear sounds of the Quran and of *dhikr*, emanating forth like the humming of bees. Even under the most difficult circumstances, the Noble Messenger ﷺ would teach them the Quran.

According to the narration of Anas ؓ, Abu Talha ؓ one day went next to the Blessed Prophet ﷺ, who was on his feet, teaching the Students of Suffa some Quran. Tied to his belly was a stone, to straighten his back, which had been bent and deplete from severe hunger. (Abu Nuaym, Hilya, I, 342)

43. Bkz. Buhârî, Nikâh, 6, 32, 35; Fedâilü'l-Kur'ân, 21, 22; Müslim, Nikâh, 76.

All their desires and pursuits were directed to understanding and learning the Book of Allah, always preoccupied with its repeated hearing and reciting.

Consequent upon them taking the Blessed Prophet ﷺ as example, the town of Medina became teeming with scholars and *huffaz*, people who had committed the entire Quran to memory.

Such was the Age of Bliss.

One wonders, if all specialists in the fields of psychology, sociology, social anthropology, pedagogy, social engineering and philosophy were to join forces, whether they could conjure a small society endowed with a blend of virtues that could even come close to the society of the Age of Bliss...Impossible! Even Farabi's work *Madinat'ul-Fadila*, the Virtuous Town, a project reflecting over an ideal society, is now left in the maws of termite, as their prey...

Touching Hymns of Prophetic Love

The one and only font of mercy and love that takes one to the ocean of Divine Love is the Blessed Prophet ﷺ. To love and to obey him is to love Allah, glory unto Him; likewise, rebelling against him is tantamount to rebelling against the Almighty.

Allah declares in the Quran:

"Say: If you love Allah then follow me and Allah will love you and forgive you your faults. Allah is Forgiving, Merciful." (Ali Imran, 31)

Directly following لاَ إِلَهَ إِلاَّ الله (There is no God but Allah) in the Word of *Tawhid* in the professing of faith are the words مُحَمَّدٌ رَسُولُ الله, (Muhammad is His Messenger). Each Word of *Tawhid*, every *salawat* in loving remembrance of the Blessed Prophet ﷺ is an investment toward the nearness and love of the Real. It is through the investment of His love that the joy of both worlds is acquired, that all spiritual conquests are obtained. The universe is a manifestation of Divine Love, the core essence of which is the Light of Muhammad, the love of whom is the only road to reaching the Essence of the Divine.

The spirituality that infuses deeds of worship, the elegance that pervades behavior, the courtesy that governs morals, the delicacy of the heart, the beauty shone upon appearance, the exquisite charm of languages, the grace that permeates feelings, the profundity of gazes, and in short, all beauties are but sparkles of the love of that Light of Being ﷺ mirrored unto hearts.

Gracefully depicted, this is, by Mawlana Rumi:

"*Come, o heart, to the real festival that is union with Muhammad...for the light you see in the universe is but a glow from the face of that blessed person.*"

It is for that reason that abidance by the exemplary ways of the Noble Messenger ﷺ is an inevitable means for attaining the love and pleasure of the Almighty. Becoming an *insan'ul-kamil*, the 'perfect human' which Islam aims towards raising, will forever remain out of reach for a Believer, who shrinks back from covering distance on the path of the Sunnah of the Great Prophet ﷺ. Neither will he achieve the true peace and bliss of the religion. Allah, glory unto Him, exhibited the archetype of the 'perfect human' in the person of the Noble Prophet ﷺ, rendering him a mercy for all being and a quintessential example for Believers.

Then how important an abidance must it be that Allah has specified it as a condition for loving His servants?

This sublime feeling undoubtedly begins with a sincere, a genuine love of the Messenger of Allah ﷺ, from the bottom of the heart, and seeking to be granted a share from his richness of heart. With regard to obeying him, our sole *uswat'ul-hasanah*, Allah, glory unto Him, declares, through the verses of the Quran:

"So take what the Messenger assigns to you, and deny yourselves that which he withholds from you; and fear Allah, for Allah is strict in punishment." (al-Hashr, 7)

"O Believers! Obey Allah and obey the Messenger, and render not your actions vain. " (Muhammad, 33)

"And whoever obeys Allah and the Messenger, these are with those upon whom Allah has bestowed favors from among the prophets and the truthful and the martyrs and the good; and a goodly company are they! " (an-Nisa, 69)

The Quran, a Divine proclamation revealed by the Almighty, has just as well been exhibited straight from the inner world of the Noble Prophet ﷺ. To be sure, the mysteries of the Sacred Book, too, are exposed to the extent one becomes enshrouded in the spirituality of the Messenger of Allah ﷺ. If, like the Companions, we become honoured with access into that world to delightfully gaze at the manifestations of Divine beauties, wisdoms underlying the permissible and the impermissible as well as those of knowledge; or to put it more bluntly, if we are able to read the Divine Word with the manifestations and glosses as have transpired within the climes of the Prophet's ﷺ heart, only then will we able to become, just like the Companions of the Age of Bliss, moths around the flame of his love, taste the ecstasy, devotion and love, in exclaiming, like the Companions, to his every command, word or even gesture:

"May my mother, father…my belongings, even my life be sacrificed to you, Messenger of Allah…"

The gracious existence of the Prophet ﷺ is, for humann kind, an object of love and a source of inspiration. The wise know that the reason for being for the whole of existence is the love it fosters for the Light of Muhammad ﷺ. The whole universe, therefore, is virtually dedicated to the Muhammad Mustafa ﷺ, the Light of Being; it has been created in his honour, as a wrapping for his light. Such a personality he is that Allah, glory unto Him, has labelled him His "Beloved".[44]

Bliss for those Believers who nurture sincere affection for Allah and His Messenger and adhere to them with love, of a kind that they hold aloft above all other kinds of love…

Gaining closeness to the Truth of Muhammad ﷺ is not so much through reason than it is with love and affection.

The skies of the month of Rabiulawwal, in which he graced the universe, were opened as a mercy and compassion for Believers.

According to sources, another of the fortunate women to have been the foster mother of the Noble Prophet ﷺ was Suwaybah, the slave of Abu Lahab, the Prophet's uncle and staunch enemy.

When Suwaybah heralded the news of the blessed birth, Abu Lahab, out of reasons purely clannish freed her as a reward. (Halabi, I, 138) Even a joy instigated by clannish patriotism was enough to alleviate Abu Lahab's torment on every Monday evening, as explained below by Abbas ؓ :

"A year following his death, I saw my brother Abu Lahab in a dream. He was in a horrid state.

'How were you treated?' I asked him.

'For freeing Suwaybah out of celebration for Muhammad's birth', he told me, 'my torment is lightened, every Monday. On

44. See, Tirmidhî, Manâqib, 1/3616; Dârimî, Muqaddima, 8; Ahmad, VI, 241; Haythamî, IX, 29.

that day I am freshened with some water that springs forth from the small hole between my thumb and index finger.'"[45]

Ibn Jazari comments:

"If the torment of an enemy of the Prophet of the calibre of Abu Lahab is alleviated simply for the joy he showed on the day of the Prophet's birth, actuated solely by feelings tribal, one must ponder on the unimaginable kinds of generous blessings awaiting a believer, who from respect to the night of the Prophet's birth, opens the feast of his heart for the love of the Eternal Grace of the Universe. What must be done, during the month of the blessed birth, is to revive enthusiasm by engaging in spiritual talks, to arrange feasts for fellow believers in order to make the most of the concealed blessings of the month, to mend broken hearts by doing all sorts of good to the poor, orphans, the lonesome and the helpless, to make them happy by handing them charity, and to read and listen to the Quran..."

The Companions' Love of the Prophet of Allah ﷺ

The Noble Prophet had endeared himself to the Companions to such a deep extent that its profundity is simply incommunicable. Such love, which is otherwise impossible, can only be established through Divine Love and inspiration.

Like a fortress knit with love, the Companions had formed a tight bond of loyalty around the Messenger of Allah ﷺ, becoming stars in the skies of his abidance, so great, that among them there were those who, in order to breathe in the

45. Ibn Kathîr, *al-Bidâya,* Cairo 1993, II, 277; Ibn Sad, I, 108, 125.

zest of abiding by him, walked the path he walked, stopped where he stopped and smelt the rose he smelt, simply because he had done those very things.

Expressions of the epic love felt by the Companions for the Blessed Prophet ﷺ are innumerable. Provided below are just a few examples:

The honourable Aisha used to describe the beauty of the Prophet's ﷺ countenance as:

وَلَوْ سَمِعَ أَهْلُ مِصْرَ أَوْصَافَ خَدِّهِ
لَمَا بَذَلُوا فِي سَوْمِ يُوسُفَ مِنْ نَقْدٍ
لَوَائِمُ زُلَيْخَا لَوْ رَأَيْنَ جَبِينَهُ
لَآثَرْنَ بِالْقَطْعِ الْقُلُوبَ عَلَى الأَيْدِ

"Had the folk of Egypt heard of His beauty,
In the bargain for Yusuf they would not have spent a dime,
Had those who condemned Zulayha seen His face,
Not their hands but their hearts would have been put to knife..."

As is evident in the Word of *Tawhid*, the Noble Prophet ﷺ is certainly a "servant" insofar as he is human, though in essence, he is "the peak of prophets". The great Aziz Mahmud Hudayi gives poetic articulation to his experience of gazing at the realm of these mysteries:

The universe is a mirror, by the Truth all things hold,
From the Mirror of Muhammad is seen Allah, behold...

The Blessed Prophet ﷺ is the centre of the manifestation of Divine Love, which develops worldly, metaphorical loves, evolving them to greatness. The moment a believer begins to tremble before the spiritual presence of the Blessed Prophet ﷺ and sense inexpressibly beautiful feelings budding in his heart, and empties his soul of all appearances and silhouettes belonging to the self, is surely when he is on the way of becoming one with him, of acquiring a share of his love.

"*Both worlds were created for one heart. Think of the meaning of the expression 'Were it not for you, I would not have created the universe'*", says Mawlana Rumi –quddisa sirruh-.

For that reason is the love of the Messenger of Allah ﷺ is the greatest means to granting one honor in both worlds and in honor of their unfathomable love for the Prophet did the Companions soar to high ranks.

Below is another of those numerous scenes from the matchless love of the Companions:

On the way to the Cave of Sawr on the journey of Hegira, Abu Bakr ؓ was walking behind the Prophet ﷺ one moment and in front of him the next.

"*Why are you walking like that?*" the Prophet ﷺ asked Abu Bakr ؓ, noticing his distinct manner.

"I fear the idolaters may catch up to you from behind, which is when I walk from behind you", said Abu Bakr ؓ. "And when I think they may be staking out ahead of you, I then quickly move in front of you."

It was evening when they eventually arrived at the mouth of the Cave.

"Please wait here until I clean out the Cave, Messenger of Allah", Abu Bakr ﷺ told him. He then meticulously sorted out the Cave, checking for holes, blocking them one by one with some fabric he instinctively ripped off from his clothes. He ended up using his entire shroud in blocking the holes, leaving all but one, which he used the sole of his foot to block.

"You can now come inside, Messenger of Allah."

Realizing the situation in the morning, the Noble Prophet asked amazedly:

"*Where is your shroud, Abu Bakr?*"

Abu Bakr ﷺ recounted what had happened the evening before. Immensely touched by his act of great magnanimity, the Messenger of Allah ﷺ lifted his hands and prayed for him.[46]

Likewise, so moving is the devotion felt for the Prophet ﷺ by a woman, whose husband, father and two sons were martyred at the battlefield of Uhud:

'Muhammad has been killed!' was the dreadful news that shook the skies of Medina on the day of Uhud, with screams of panic reaching the heavens. Everyone had poured out onto the streets, in hope of receiving some news from those coming in to the town. Even though Sumayra ﷺ, an Ansari woman, had received the terrible news that her husband, two sons and father had all been slain martyred at the field of Uhud, she had little taken heed; her mind preoccupied with the real anxiety, her heart racing for the wellbeing of the Messenger of Allah ﷺ:

"Is *he* all right?" she was repeatedly asking.

46. See, Ibn Kathîr, *al-Bidâya*, III, 222-223; Ali al-Qârî, *Mirkât*, Beirut 1992, X, 381-382/6034; Abû Nuaym, *Hily*, I, 33.

"*Alhamdulillah* he is alive and well", the incoming Companions were answering, "just as you wish he is."

"My heart will not rest at ease until I see him. Show me the Messenger of Allah", she then replied, still nervous.

When they did show her the Blessed Prophet ﷺ, the courageous Sumayra raced towards him and grabbing hold of the edge of his shirt exclaimed:

"May my parents be sacrificed for you, Messenger of Allah! So long as you are alive, nothing can make me worry me anymore." (Waqidi, I, 292; Haythami, VI, 115)

Anas ibn Malik رضي الله عنه narrates:

"A man came to the Messenger of Allah ﷺ and asked:

'When will the Day of Judgment arrive?'

'*What have you prepared for the Day of Judgment?*' asked the Prophet ﷺ in return.

'The love of Allah and His Messenger', responded the man.

Thereupon the Messenger of Allah ﷺ told him:

'*Then you shall be with whom you love...*'"

Commenting on his narration, Anas رضي الله عنه then adds:

"Apart from entering Islam, nothing has made us happier than the words of the Messenger of Allah '*you shall be with whom you love*'. And I myself, too, love Allah and His Messenger, and Abu Bakr and Omar; and though I have not been able to match what they have done, I expect to be with them." (Muslim, Birr, 163)

Undeniably, in order to find a place within the encouraging promise made by the Noble Prophet ﷺ, each believer must embellish his heart with the Prophet's ﷺ love and inspiring light.

At the time of the passing away of the Blessed Messenger ﷺ, the Companions were like candles melting from the flame of grief. That day, from separation from the Great Friend ﷺ, hearts had suddenly scorched from the fires of longing, and Companions were flung from one distraught state to another. Even Omar ؓ had for a moment lost consciousness, struggling under pangs of great intensity, until Abu Bakr ؓ eventually stood and calmed people down. Loving hearts, which could not resist not seeing him even for a day, would now no longer be able to see the Noble Prophet ﷺ with in this life. Unable to bear this pain for much longer, the broken-hearted Abdullah ibn Zayd ؓ lifted his hands to the Almighty and prayed entreatingly:

"Allah...Blind my eyes! Do not let me see anything of the world after the Prophet whom I loved more than anyone else!" His prayer, amid the downpour of sincere tears, was granted and he became blind there and then.[47]

Thereafter, whenever Abu Bakr ؓ attempted to narrate a hadith of the Blessed Prophet ﷺ, memories of him would reduce him to tears, finding it difficult to even utter a word.

Describing his condition is Abu Hurayra ؓ:

"Abu Bakr ؓ once ascended the pulpit and said:

47. Qurtubî, *al-Jâmî,* Beirut 1985, V, 271.

'As you know, the Messenger of Allah had last year stood where I am standing now and…' He began to cry, unable to continue. He then repeated these words, but once again cried. He tried for the third time, only to be reduced to tears once again." (See, Tirmidhi, Daawat, 105/3558; Ahmad, I, 3)

Despite always being by the side of the Prophet ﷺ in his life, Abu Bakr ؓ would constantly miss him; and after the Prophet's ﷺ passing away, the longing became fiercer, aggravated with the desire to join him.

The honorable Aisha elaborates the excitement her father felt at the time of his death to unite with the Blessed Messenger ﷺ:

"My father Abu Bakr asked, on his deathbed:

'What day is it today?'

'Monday', we told him.

'If I die tonight', he then said, 'do not wait tomorrow for my burial…for the most favorite time for me is that which is nearest to my reunion with the Messenger of Allah ﷺ.'" (Ahmad, I, 8)

Among the Companions were those who would be envious of the ill, thinking their long awaited reunion with their beloved Messenger ﷺ would be now imminent now that they were lying on their deathbeds, and would send their greetings to the Sultan of the Hearts ﷺ with them. Muhammad ibn Munqadir ؓ, just to name one, had visited Jabir ؓ, a Companion immersed in the love of the Prophet ﷺ, during his final illness. Realizing his death was pending, to console Jabir ؓ, heartsick from longing for the Prophet ﷺ, he remarked:

"Send my greeting to the Messenger of Allah…" (Ibn Majah, Janaiz, 4)

The Companions, the devoted lovers of the Prophet of Allah ﷺ, would take great pleasure in listening to recollections of him.

Bara ؓ recounts his father's ingrained desire to listen to a memory of the Messenger of Allah ﷺ whenever the slightest opportunity presented itself:

"Abu Bakr as-Siddiq ؓ had bought a saddle from my father for thirteen dirhams, before requesting:

'Tell Bara to deliver it to our house if he can.'

'No way', my father said. 'Not until you tell me how you made the Hegira from Mecca to Medina with the Messenger of Allah ﷺ with the idolaters behind your trail!'

Abu Bakr ؓ then recapped the journey in the following:

'We left the Cave and began to move. We walked all night and the following day. Come noon, I took a look around with the hope of perhaps finding a shade. Nearby I saw a rock with some shade. I quickly leveled the ground under the shade and laid out a mantle for the Messenger of Allah ﷺ to sit.

'Please, Messenger of Allah,' I said. 'Have some rest.'

The Prophet of Allah ﷺ resigned for a little rest. I began looking around to see whether anyone was coming. What I saw instead was a shepherd, steering his sheep towards the rock. Like I a moment ago, he too was searching for shade.

'Whose shepherd are you?' I asked him. He gave a name from Quraysh, a person I knew.

'Do the sheep have milk?' I then inquired.

'Yes' he replied.

'Then can you milk us some? I asked him.[48]

'Of course I can', he said, 'with pleasure...'

He then swiftly got hold of a sheep from the herd. I told him to thoroughly clean his hands and the sheep's breasts. He cleaned his hands by striking them, rubbing them together, before milking the sheep awhile and then handing me the milk. I had been carrying with me a leather bottle, for the Messenger of Allah ﷺ, which I had closed off with a piece of cloth. I poured some water from it on the milk, which cooled it down somewhat. I presented it to the Messenger of Allah ﷺ. He had just awoken from a nap.

'Please, Messenger of Allah...Have some milk', I said.

He drank the milk. Only then did I feel somewhat at ease...'" (Bukhari, Ashab'un-Nabi, 2; Ahmad, I, 2)

The Companions felt so great a love and respect for the Blessed Prophet ﷺ that there were some who would not cut their hair simply because the Prophet's ﷺ hands had touched it. (Abu Dawud, Salat, 28/501)

48. Arab custom regarded the milk of all livestock to be permissible for travelers. Stock owners would ensure the shepherds they hired did not prevent any wayfarers passing by from helping themselves to the milk of the herd. Judging in accordance with custom is an accepted part of the methodology of Islamic jurisprudence. (Suhayli, Ravd'ul-Unuf, Beirut, 1978, II, 152) The Messenger of Allah ﷺ states: "*There are three groups of people with whom Allah shall not speak in the Hereafter: those who withhold the excess water they have from a traveler, those who after asr give false oath just to sell their goods and those who pledge allegiance to the Caliph, then keep their word if the Caliph provides for them and turning back on their heels if he does not.*" (Abu Dawud, Buyu', 60/3474)

A beautiful manifestation of love indeed, is the following account bearing the way in which female Companions instilled the love of the Blessed Messenger ﷺ in their children; women who would scold them when they would delay, for too long a time, seeing the Messenger of Allah ﷺ. One of them was Huzayfa ؓ, admonished by his mother for not having seen the Prophet ﷺ for a few days. Huzayfa ؓ himself recounts:

"My mother asked me of the last time I had seen the Messenger of Allah ﷺ. 'It has been a few days', I told her.

She told me off, rebuking me severely.

'Don't be mad', I said. 'I will go to the Messenger of Allah ﷺ at once and perform the *maghrib* salat with him, and ask him to pray for forgiveness for both you and I.'" (Tirmidhi, Manaqib, 30/3781; Ahmad, V, 391-392)

The condition of Bilal ؓ, the chief *muaddhin* of the Prophet's mosque, was something else. Once the Messenger of Allah ﷺ departed the world, he virtually lost his tongue; even the sharpest of knives could not part his lips. Despite all her enormity Medina had grown small in his eyes.

In reminiscence of the sweet memories of the *adhan*s of the time of the Blessed Prophet ﷺ, Caliph Abu Bakr ؓ pleaded Bilal ؓ on numerous occasions to recite the *adhan* once again for old time's sake. Instead, the distressed Bilal ؓ would ask to be pardoned.

"If you ask how I feel, Abu Bakr, I have lost all power to call the *adhan* after the passing away of the Messenger of Allah...So please, leave me to myself."

But Abu Bakr ؓ was committed to rehear the *adhan* of the sweet times gone by.

"As if the loss of their Prophet is bearable, do you wish to deprive the *ummah* of his *muaddhin* too?"

Yielding to the adamant requests, Bilal ﷺ finally made his way up the minaret one morning, at dawn, downcast and teary eyed, to call the *adhan* for *fajr* salat; though overcome with emotion, he made his way back down, unable to keep his voice from choking, unable to do the call. Abu Bakr ﷺ insisted no more.

Bilal ﷺ could not remain in Medina any longer, a town evoking vivid memories of the Blessed Prophet ﷺ at every corner, and immediately after the *fajr* salat that morning, he left for Damascus. Infused with the hope of reuniting with his beloved Prophet ﷺ, he took active part in battles in the frontiers, one after another, with martyrdom eluding him every time however, much to his disappointment. Years had gone by. In spite of the plague that laid waste to Damascus claiming twenty-five thousand lives, Divine decree had again spared Bilal ﷺ from breathing his last, his heart ever burning amid the scorching fire of separation.

One day he saw the Messenger of Allah ﷺ in his dream.

"*How long must this separation last, Bilal?*" he was telling him, with grievance. "*Isn't it time you visited me?*"

Distressed, Bilal ﷺ suddenly woke up. Without further ado, he left, this time to visit the hallowed grave of the Noble Prophet ﷺ in Medina. Just as he was bowling his eyes out in the presence of his beloved, shedding tears on his grave, Hasan and Husain arrived. Elated to see the dear grandsons of the Noble Prophet ﷺ, who used to treasure them as 'the sweet basils' of paradise, Bilal ﷺ warmly hugged them.

"We would love to hear you call the *adhan*, Bilal", they pleaded, and to their wish Bilal ﷺ succumbed. His *adhan* shook Medina. When he came to the part *Ashadu anna Muhammadan Rasulullah*, all the men and women of the town took to the streets and began pouring into the Mosque, thinking the Noble Prophet ﷺ had come back to life. Since the passing away of the Blessed Prophet ﷺ, never had there been a day in which the dwellers of Medina shed more tears.[49]

The celebrated Companion, a genuine devotee of the Prophet ﷺ, ultimately passed away in Damascus. He was over sixty at the time.

Right before his death, it is reported that he was jovially exclaiming, "Tomorrow, Allah willing, I shall reunite with my dear friends…the Messenger of Allah and his companions."

His wife mourning the looming death of her husband in the background, Bilal ﷺ, in the meantime, was expressing joy, murmuring, "How wonderful…" (Dhahabi, Siyar, I, 359)

The exuberant love of the Companions for the Prophet of Mercy ﷺ can equally be seen in their narration hadith. Apprehensive of unknowingly making a mistake while conveying the words of the Prophet ﷺ, it was not uncommon for them to shake in the knees and turn pale. Abdullah ibn Masud ﷺ, for one, would begin to violently tremble the moment he would begin to quote the Blessed Messenger ﷺ. In consideration of their perceived weaknesses, after quoting the Messenger of Allah ﷺ, many Companions would be quick to tentatively specify, "…he either said that or something along those lines." (Ibn Majah, Muqaddimah, 3)

49. Ibn Esîr, *Usdü'l-Ghaba,* I, 244-245; Dhahabî, *Siyaru A'lâm'in-Nubelâ*, Beirut 1986-1988, I, 357-358.

Such a grand Prophet he was that the date log on which he would give the sermon would moan from his longing. For his thirsty *ummah*, his fingers became fonts from which they quenched their thirst. The ill, who took sips from the bowl from which he had taken *wudu*, found cure. Those eating with him heard the invocations of morsels.[50] *Sakal-ı Şerif*, the hallowed strands of his hair and beard, has been kept in mosques to this day, cherished as part of his loving legacy.

The leader of the plain of resurrection in the Hereafter is Him…

To intercede for sinners is Him,

Weeping *ummatii, ummatii* (*my ummah, my ummah*) is Him,

The Flag of the *Liwa'ul-Hamd* of the Hereafter rests in His hands,

All prophets are under His shade,

The hands that will open, for the first time, the doors of Paradise, are again His…

Vibrantly depicting this scene is Sheikh Galib:

On the pulpit of the eternal climes, your sermon is read
In the Trial of the Final Court, your verdict is kept
Your gulbang'i qudum[51] *is shouted upon the Throne,*
Mentioned is your noble name in the Heavens and Earth

---

50. For that and similar miracles see, Bukhârî, Manâqib, 25.
51. *Gülbâng-i kudûm* is the prayer or the ceremonial chant collectively recited in the company of religious music, or the ceremonial welcoming and praises said in tribute of the arrival of a person.

The Fountain of Love after the Companions

The convoy of love and affection for the Blessed Prophet ﷺ, a mercy encompassing all worlds, continued with the same enthusiasm, following the Companions, to flow like a blustery torrent towards the ocean of reunion, fully conscious that only through loving the Prophet ﷺ would the peace and bliss of both worlds be obtained.

The Messenger of Allah ﷺ has foretold that his lovers will not cease until the Final Hour:

"*Some of the most to love me, among my ummah, shall be from among those that will appear after me. To see me, they are eagerly prepared to forfeit their families and belongings.*" (Muslim, Jannat, 12; Hakim, IV, 95/6991)

May Allah, glory unto Him, include us, His helpless slaves, amongst those praised in the hadith!

Amin..

The below heartrending account, recounted by Abdullah ibn Mubarak, reveals that the love of the Noble Prophet ﷺ transcends all pains mortal:

"I was next to Imam Malik, who was narrating some of the hadith of the Messenger of Allah ﷺ. But that he was in agony could be seen in his face. However much he may have been turning pale by the moment, he still continued conveying the Prophet's words regardless. Once the lesson was over and the students disbanded, I said to him:

'Abu Abdullah...There seems to be something strange about you today.'

'Yes', he replied. 'A scorpion came from nowhere and bit me several times during the lesson. But I held out from my reverence for the Messenger of Allah ﷺ.'"[52]

Out of respect for the ground walked by the Noble Prophet ﷺ, Imam Malik never rode a camel or a horse within Medina; neither did he wear any shoes. Whenever a visitor would arrive by his door with the intent of clearing a query with regard to a hadith, from esteem of the words of the Blessed Messenger ﷺ, he would first take *wudu*, wrap an *imamah* around his head, put on some sweet fragrances and sit on a high stool; only then would he accept the visitor. He would thereby prepare himself spiritually for the grace of the Noble Prophet ﷺ, taking utmost care to observe the manners suitable for conveying his words. The Imam always spoke with a low voice at the *Rawdah*, the area between the pulpit and the blessed grave of the Prophet ﷺ at the Mosque of Medina; and so was quick to caution Abu Jafar Mansur, the Caliph of then, who momentarily raised his voice there:

"Lower your voice in this area, Caliph. Allah's warning not to raise one's voice in the presence of the Messenger of Allah was revealed to a group much virtuous than you..."

Imam Malik, again, forgave the Governor of Medina who had caused him unjustified troubles, remarking:

"I would feel embarrassed to seek my rights in the Hereafter from an offspring of the Prophet of Allah ﷺ."

Among the notables of the *ummah* celebrated for their loving devotion to the Prophet of Mercy ﷺ, Sayyid Ahmad

52. Münâwî, *Fayzü'l-Qadîr,* Beirut 1994, III, 333; Suyutî, *Miftâhu'l-Jannah,*, p. 52.

Yasawi, stemming from his profound love, bade farewell to living above the ground after he turned sixty-three, the age in which the Messenger of Allah ﷺ had passed away, and for ten years until his death, continued his life of calling people to the true path, from a grave like place below the ground.

The great scholar of hadith Imam Nawawi similarly never ate a watermelon in his life, for the sole reason that he did not know the manner in which the Blessed Prophet ﷺ had eaten it.

A saint who could provide a stepping stone to elevating one to the reality of the Gracious Prophet ﷺ, was perceived by Yavuz Sultan Selim, incidentally a world emperor, above anything else on Earth, a feeling to which he gives voice in the below couplet placing a yearning accent on attaining closeness to the friends of Allah and His Messenger:

Being a sultan to the world, it turns out, is a scuffle, boring,
But being a disciple to a saint is superior to the whole thing...

There was a custom, in times bygone, of engraving a couplet or a quotation in seals. In elaboration of how the Almighty created the universe in honor of His love for the Light of Muhammad, Bezmi Alem Valide Sultan had the ode below engraved in her seal:

From love, was Muhammad born,
Without Muhammad...love is forlorn
From its manifestation did Bazm-i Alam befall...

The fire is depicted by Fuzuli in his legendary *Su Kasidesi* as follows:

Do not shed, my eyes, your water of love for my hearts fire,
For flames so rampantly rising, there is no cure in water

Perplexed, my eyes do not know wherefrom the skies get their color,
Have my tears pervaded the skies or has it really the color of water?

From watering the rose garden let not the gardener bother
A rose like His face won't bloom, even if a thousand, he were to water

With my wish unfulfilled of kissing His hand, my friends, if I expire
Cast a pot from my soil and with it present to my beloved some water

All their lives, dashing their heads against one rock to another,
To reach the grounds He walked, like a drifter, flows water

"An extraordinary light which even the sun orbits", a poetic remark belonging to Suleyman Çelebi, who conceives even the sun as revolving around the Great Prophet ﷺ.

Sultan Ahmed had an image of the footprints of the Noble Prophet ﷺ copied onto his turban, with the intent of receiving inspiration from what it evoked, under which he wrote the poem:

What if I carried above my head, like a crown,
...The pure feet of the Sultan of Prophets?
Of the Prophets garden, he is the Rose after all,
So be crowned, Ahmed, with the soles of that Rose

The same love is articulated by Aziz Mahmud Hudayi as:

Your arrival is a mercy, a blissful pleasure,
A cure for the lovesick, Prophet, is your sight,
Grant intercession to Hudayi, be it inner or outer,

Curled by your door, he is a slave in plight

En route to Pilgrimage, with Medina visible from a distance, poet Nabi was deeply upset to see a pasha (army general) unknowingly stretch his feet out towards the Sacred *Rawdah*. Grief-stricken, he put pen to paper to write the poem below giving voice to his reverence of the Blessed Prophet ﷺ:

Desist from disrespect; this is the land of the Lords Beloved,
The focus of Divine view, this is the site of the Prophet,

Enter this shrine, Nabi, intent only on utmost conduct,
The busegah[53] *of Prophets this is, the precincts of the sacred...*

As a consequence of the sincere inspiration that flowed directly from Nabi's heart, with the miraculous signal of the Messenger of Allah ﷺ, the *muadhhins* of the Rawdah recited the poem aloud from the minarets during the salat of *fajr*. Nabi, extremely moved by the emotional sight, entered the Mosque teary eyed.

M. Esad Effendi, among the greatest sheikhs of late, lyrically describes how he is reduced to ashes amid the smouldering flames of the Prophet's love:

From your spellbinding appearance, my love, spring is on fire,

On fire is the rose, the nightingale, the hyacinth, soil and spine...on fire

Burning all lovers is but the rays of your beaming face,
On fire is the tongue, the heart, eyes crying from your love... on fire

How is it possible to cleanse the martyrs of love with all this fire?

53. A *busegah* denotes any given spot that receives kisses.

On fire is the body, the shroud, the sweet water for cleansing... on fire

The touching poet of late, formerly a Christian who adopted the name Yaman Dede after experiencing the zest of the Muhammedan Light, becoming an emotional believer and a loving devotee of the Blessed Prophet ﷺ, articulates the beautiful poem below:

I would feel no pain if thirsting in a scorching desert, I breathed my last

I feel no dampness in oceans, in my heart volcanoes blast,

If the skies rained flames, barely would I feel its glaze,

Relief through your beautiful appearance, o Prophet, for I am ablaze

To pass away on your lap with your love, what ecstasy it would be,

To die in your chamber, my lord, is it really that unlikely?

They will feel safe from harm dying in your love, as my eyes give way,

Relief through your beautiful appearance, o Prophet, for I am ablaze

Brokenhearted, I am deplete, with you is the cure for my concern,

Scorched from fire, my lips murmur your name around your throne,

Bless this poor nobody whenever your heart pleases, make his day

Relief through your beautiful appearance, o Prophet, for I am ablaze

Kemâl Edib Kürkçüoğlu gives eloquent voice to the excitement and exhilaration of the heavens occasioned by the *Miraj*, the Ascension, of the Prophet ﷺ thereto:

At the night of Miraj for staring at his face,
To the ground, in gratitude, heavens fall prostrate

Excitedly wearing his ihram every evening,
The Holy Spirit aches to enter as guest through his gate

Whoever sees once, screams 'Allah Allah', hoping,
With their minds lost, to see again his face...

Such a character is the Messenger of Allah ﷺ that everyone to have accepted him as the guide and followed him has become unique personalities in their own rights, like the stars in the skies. The Companions, the friends of the Truth and the righteous were able to gain virtue and worth only to the extent of their closeness to that Great Light of Being ﷺ.

How much of a share do we have, one cannot help but wonder, of the inner feelings of Abdullah ibn Zayd, Bilal Habashi, Imam Nawawi, Sayyid Ahmed Yesevi and the likes? Within the framework of the love manifest since the Companions, we too must measure our love for the Prophet ﷺ, weigh the extent in which we are worthy of being his *ummah* and inject a dose of spiritual revival, an awakening in our souls.

The distinguished Muslim notables aforementioned are, to be sure, embodiments of the highest standards, as lofty as the stars. But what has made them stars in the skies of Muslim hearts is the intensity of their love and devotion for the Prophet ﷺ.

Love, we know, is like an electric current between two hearts. To be a Believer true to the spirit it is vital to acquire the heart this capacity. The trauma haunting contemporary humankind is simply a consequence of the loss of this capacity of the heart, a tragedy that lays waste to many a great potential, crushing it under the hammer of the ego; and when inclinations are always worldly and egotistic, nobody seems to be able to find a way in reinvigorating the spirit. The elevation to Real Love from that which is metaphorical, for Majnun to at long last reach his Lord in a journey that begun with Layla, is possible through the maturation of a crude heart, through exercise, and its gaining the capacity for that Real Love, of which humankind today is in desperate need. All the evil, the atrocities and the crudeness so rampant is because of a lack of *love*.

The greatness of a love is measured by the sacrifice made for the beloved, when the need arises, and the risk taken. A true lover can sacrifice his life, if need be, without even thinking to have made a sacrifice at all; he rather moves calmly, as if paying a debt. Those ignorant of real love and unable to seize a share have effectively desisted entering the path of maturation, preferring to abide by the domination of their egos, squandering their hearts, laying it on the path of waste.

Acceptance of the *amanah*, the trust, from which even the mountains recoiled, is in fact a privilege granted by the Almighty to humankind. The precondition of having this privilege lies in reaching real love. Only in real love does the conflict and battle raging in the soul of man melt away and perish. A mature person, through the inspiring reflections acquired from an exemplary character, rids his soul of bestial inclinations and turns his heart into a garden of paradise, in which windows are opened for the viewing of Divine spectacles.

"…**I breathed from my Spirit**", (al-Hijr, 29) states our Lord in the Quran, reminding the sublime essence, of His Own, He gave man. Once that sublime essence is allowed, through love, to usher a Believer to maturation, then the heart begins to cover distance towards the realm of Divine mysteries, revealed in which is the truth of matter, the gist of man and the universe. One is then granted the manifestations of a pure heart.

When one reaches that level of maturation, curtains of ignorance, hitherto separating the servant from his Lord, are parted, and meted out is a share of the secret 'to die before death'. The world, its fleeting love and all its passing pomp is then removed from the sight, discarded from the heart. The spirit, then, indulges in the inexpressible zest of gaining closeness to its Maker.

Those who have not tasted real love have been unable to shatter the bestial frame surrounding man and take a step inside the angelic realm. The heart of one who does not know how to love is akin to raw soil. Love is the abode of wisdom, insofar as it is the reason for being.

The Divine Mercy necessary to accompany humanity if it is to take a leap from depravity to bliss is the Messenger of Allah ﷺ, presented as a quintessential example for mankind. The path to real happiness is paved upon learning real love from him, in becoming annihilated in his character and following his unswerving lead with such love.

The Blessed Prophet ﷺ is the Beloved of the entire universe and the reason for its existence. He is a guide of union between the Lord and the servant. With a sublime series of conduct, both those that are communicable and those that elude even the most articulate of descriptions, until his very last breath, the Noble Messenger ﷺ has for us provided the best example of being a servant to the Real.

In short, he is a mercy and a love that encompasses the entire realms of existence. Hearts aching for him in this universe will forever burn with his love, inhaling with every breath the air of a long awaited reunion; and amid these flames of the heart, they will plead:

"Relief through your beautiful appearance, for I am burning o Prophet", a cry through which they will give vent to a love intensifying by the moment.

It is this love that has rendered the likes of Bahauddin Naqshiband, Yunus and Mawlana Rumi the sparkling stars of the spiritual skies. It was with this love that Mawlana Rumi took a step inside the real and the eternal climes of happiness; a happiness that was reunion with the Eternal, the Supreme. Insofar as they covered distance towards eternity by virtue of slipping away from the captivity of the mortal flesh, nothing short of the Eternal would have pleased them. After all, how could real happiness, everlasting, blend with the mortal, afflicted with impermanence? The road towards the blissful clime passes through surrendering love and affection to its deserved place.

The subsequent words of Mawlana Rumi, in a sense, reveal the source of his joy:

"So long as I am alive, I am at the service of the Quran, a dust on the path of Muhammad ﷺ. I am distant from the person, and his words, who conveys a word other than that what I say."

The gist of becoming a dust on the path of the Noble Messenger ﷺ and devotedly adhering to his path is a lifelong loving abidance by him and obeying the Sunnah in all matters great and small.

Another way of acquiring the required blend in abiding by the Light of Being ﷺ and becoming enshrouded in his spirituality is to keep the *salawat'us-sharifah* rolling constantly of our tongues, sure to reinforce the bond of our hearts with him and inspire his dear love within.

Salawat'us-Sharifah

In the Holy Quran, Allah, glory unto Him, vows by the Prophet's ﷺ life. Mentioning his great name next to His Own, the Almighty has required belief in his prophethood, as a precondition of being a worthy servant. Allah took offense in others raising their voices in the presence of His Beloved ﷺ, cautioning against calling out his name like any other. What's more, the Almighty has stated that He and the angels send their numerous blessings, *salawat'us-sharifah*, to the Prophet ﷺ, ordering his *ummah* amply do the same.

In accordance with the *ayah*:

"**Allah and His angels send blessings on the Prophet: O Believers! Send your blessings on him and salute him with all respect**," (al-Ahzab, 56) sending *salawat'us-sharifah* to that Great Being is a duty for all Believers, laid down by Allah, glory unto Him.

Narrating the following is Ubayy ibn Kab رضي الله عنه:

"A third of the night had passed when the Messenger of Allah awoke from his sleep and said:

'*Remember Allah, people, remember Allah! Blown will be the first horn that will rattle the ground. Then will follow the second. Death will arrive with all its intensity; death will arrive with all its intensity...*'

'I send lots of *salawat'us-sharifah*, Messenger of Allah', said I. 'How often should I do it?'

'*As much as you wish*' he replied.

'Would it be right if I spared a quarter of my prayer for it?' I again inquired.

'*Spare as much from it as you wish*', he advised. '*But it will be better for you if you spared more.*'

'Then I will spare half', I proposed.

'*As you wish…But better if you spared more*', said he.

'How about I spared two-thirds then?'

'*As you wish… But better if you spared more*'.

'How would it be then if I send *salawat'us-sharifah* in the entire time I spare for prayer?' I then asked.

'*If you do*', the Messenger of Allah ﷺ replied, '*then Allah will rid you of all your troubles and forgive your sins.*'" (Tirmidhi, Qiyamat, 23/2457)

Devotees of the Prophet ﷺ, therefore, embrace the *salawat'us-sharifah* as a continuous chant, for they are means of increasing the love of the Prophet in a Believer's heart. Appropriately following the Blessed Messenger ﷺ and making the most of the quintessential example he has provided doubtless comes through a grasp of the reality of the Quran and Sunnah, which in turn is possible only by virtue of drawing closer to the exemplary morals of the Prophet ﷺ, and delving into the depths of his heart.

No mortal has succeeded in describing his essential attribute; his towering morals and disposition has eluded comprehension. The wise, those spiritual sultans, even the great Jibril, have all accepted being on his path as the greatest honor, begging by his door as the most indefinable bliss.

On another note, according to the manners of prayer advised by Islam, all prayers begin and end with thanking Allah, glory unto Him, and sending blessings to the Blessed Prophet ﷺ. There is an established conviction that Allah, glory unto Him, never turns down a *salawat'us-sharifah*, which, in essence, is a prayer and plea to the Almighty; the precise reason as to why prayers are adorned with it, both in the start and in the end. That is to say, squeezing in personal prayers amid two, whose acceptances are highly expected, is to ensure their acceptance as well.

"A prayer is left hanging between the earth and the skies," states Omar ؓ "and is not raised to Allah until blessings are sent to the Messenger of Allah ﷺ." (Tirmidhi, Witr, 21/486)

Indeed, the Noble Prophet ﷺ one day happened to see a man who, after salat, was praying without expressing thanks to Allah, glory unto Him, and sending blessings to His Messenger.

"*The man rushed it*", the Prophet ﷺ then remarked, before calling him over to give advice:

"*Upon wishing to make a prayer, one should first thank and praise Allah and send blessings to His Prophet…and then afterward continue in whichever manner desired.*" (Tirmidhi, Da'awat, 64/3477)

The importance in prayers of resorting to *tawassul*, submitting the Prophet's name ﷺ as a means, reverberates in the following incident recounted by Ibn Abbas ؓ:

"There was an ongoing war between the Jews of Khaybar and the tribe of Ghatafan, where the Jews were always routed. In the end they prayed:

'Lord...we ask for victory in the name of the Unlettered Prophet whose appearance in the Final Epoch you have avowed', after which they defeated Ghatafan. Yet, once Allah, glory unto Him, did make appear the Messenger of Allah ﷺ whose name they appealed in their prayer, the Jews rejected his prophethood and the book revealed to him; whereupon Allah proclaimed:

'**And when there came to them a Book from Allah verifying that which they have, and aforetime they used to pray for victory against those who disbelieve, but when there came to them (Prophet) that which they did not recognize, they disbelieved in him; so Allah's curse is on the unbelievers.**'" (al-Baqara, 89) (Qurtubi, II, 27; Wahidi, p. 31)

Evident is thus the fact even non-Believers were able to make use of the mercy and abundance that permeated the universe with the coming of the Prophet of Mercy ﷺ, owing to his splendid honor in Divine Sight.

Addressing the Prophet ﷺ, Allah assures:

"**But Allah will not punish them while you are with them, nor will He punish them while they seek forgiveness.**" (al-Anfal, 33)

This Divine assurance was also revealed with regard to non-Believers. Since even they are given such a privilege, simply owing to their physical proximity to the Blessed Prophet ﷺ, the blessings awaiting Believers is simply inconceivable; especially provided they not only affirm faith in the Exceptional

Being, but moreover receive a share of his love as the core of their faith. Words, here, are powerless…Beyond a shadow of a doubt, the extent of happiness in the world and the greatness of ranks in the Hereafter are to the degree of depth a Believer lets his heart immerse in the love of the Prophet ﷺ.

Therefore do not forget sending your blessings and peace to him…for you too stand in need of his intercession in the darkest of hours!

Part Four

- The Greatest Need: An Exemplary Character
- How Much Do We Love Him?

The Greatest Need for the Heart and the Mind: An Exemplary Character

The Education that Makes Man: Divine Teaching

Allah, glory unto Him, has rendered the earth and the skies to the service of human beings,[54] whom have not been left to wander irresponsibly in response to their Lord and their ambiance.[55] Expressed more clearly, the Almighty has guided both the universe and man by means of divine laws, decreeing thereby a sweet balance between freedom and responsibility in this life of trial, amplified in the verse below:

"And the sky He has uplifted; and He has set the measure, that you exceed not the measure" (ar-Rahman, 7-8)

This means that man ought to become one with the harmony prevalent in the universe. Just as there is not the least imbalance in this universe of vast proportions, humans must not give sway to the least digression on their journey towards adhering to the Almighty. Only those that are able to observe this balance for a lifetime merit being the wise, the happiest of both worlds. But those living a life of imbalance by giving rein to passing desires and short lived pleasures are simply ignorant of the mystery of coming to and passing through this

54. See, Jâthiya, 13.
55. See, Qiyamat, 36.

life, unable to become one with the Divine harmony that resonates in the universe, incapable of comprehending it. What a waste it is that their lives pass in the lure of a deep whirlpool of ignorance, a prelude to their Hereafter, an ominous and even greater dismay.

The answer to this mystery lies hidden within the reality that is the human being. One thing for certain is that sent into this world for trial, man has thus been created with a potential for both right and wrong. A trial, after all, requires that one is endowed with the power to do both.

Dominating a person's life both internally and externally, therefore, is a constant tug of war between right and wrong. Both desire control of the human frame. As much as there is an inherent power for right within, there is a power for wrong, valid for unrefined egos. Forces of reason, cognition and will alone do not suffice to aid good victory over evil in this incessant battle. Had they been enough, the Almighty would not have reinforced Adam عليه السلام the first man He created, with prophethood, and would not have revealed to him the Divine Truths that grant one the goodness of both worlds. Quite the reverse, Allah, glory unto Him, has always steered humankind to the Real, through prophets and revelation. Reinforcing both reason and the heart with revealed books, He has subjected His servants to a spiritual training.

Reason is like a two-edged sword; it can lead one to both virtue and vice. True, human beings do attain the level of *ahsanu taqwim*, the highest rank one can reach, through the aid of reason; yet more often than not, it is owing to reason that they plummet to the pits of *bal hum adall*, a level of consciousness way below even of beasts. Reason must therefore come under discipline, none other than the training of Revelation and the teaching of Prophets. Provided it is under the supervision of Revelation, reason can then lead man to the shore. Deprived of the guidance of Revelation, on the other hand, it is sure to drown in a tragic end.

History has been witness many tyrants, with sound rational capacities, who have yet not felt the slightest remorse for committing the most brutal of massacres; for they perceived their brutalities as sound, rational behavior. Hulagu Khan, for one, drowned four-hundred-thousand innocent people in the waters of Tigris, without feeling the least guilt. Before Islam, many Meccan men used to take their daughters to bury them alive, amid the silent screams of their mothers that shed their hearts to pieces. Chopping a slave was no different for them than chopping wood; they even saw it as their natural right.

They too had reason and feelings, just like us, which however were like the teeth of a wheel working the opposite direction, defiant of expectation.

Demonstrated by all this is the natural need human beings have for guidance and being directed, owing to the positive and negative inclinations and desires within. The direction given, however, must in turn be compatible with creational disposition; and this is possible only through education in the light of Revelation, that is the guidance and enlightening of prophets. Otherwise, a direction conflicting with creational disposition will only generate evil.

A feature that dominates a person's character, whatever it may be, assumes an annihilatory role of its opposite. If right dominates, it makes wrong ineffective. If wrong is given the upper hand, it then tries to suffocate right. The inner conflict thus persists for a lifetime. It is for this reason that the Almighty has additionally blessed humankind with prophets and saints, as teachers of guidance. Only those reared by those skillful and inspiring hands have been able to develop their inner beauties, turning their wintry frosts into springs of vibrant blooms. The half savage society of the Age of Ignorance, for one, were able to develop into the most cherished generation of all time, thanks to the guidance of the Blessed Prophet ﷺ.

This is for no other reason than that as long as they stick by the guiding light of prophets, people will become servants of the kind Allah is pleased with, worthy of praise. If not, they are doomed for failure in the Divine test, fought between the ego and the spirit, and plunge to the pits of the lowest. The worldly life was in fact created to establish which side human beings would decide to take. Man directs either the positive or the negative inclinations with towards one of these sides, with his own will; a directing that is decided by the result of the battle between the spirit and the ego. Yet whilst the battle is decided, meanwhile, he is exposed to many influences. A stroll through a rose garden leaves one scenting beautifully of roses; just the same, a walk through filth is also destined to smear its mark. External influences are always visible, making human beings prone as being the most in need, among entire creation, of a refining guidance and education.

Falling into depravity at the expense of laying waste to this fleeting life, stem from the inner and outer conflicts, seemingly insoluble, man experiences. These conflicts are, in essence, caused by the fact that man bears, at once, the highest of virtues that are means of gaining nearness to the Creator and the most deplorable of bestial features.

Consequently, the inner worlds of those who have not come under that training and whose hearts are therefore yet be reconciled with peace resemble forests in which numerous animals dwell. Virtually disguised under their temperaments are the natures of numerous animals. Some are as cunning as foxes, while others are as ferocious as hyenas. Some take after ants and greedily stockpile, and others are as venomous as snakes. Some caress before they bite whereas others suck blood like slugs; there are yet others that hide deceit behind a smile. Each of these are attributes peculiar to certain animals.

A person unsuccessful in breaking the domination of his ego through spiritual education, thus unable to construct a firm character is under the constant siege of such deplorable habits. Many a person is dictated by the character of a single animal, while there are an added more dominating others. Besides, as their natures reflect onto their looks, it is not so difficult pick out their hidden characters, for those who understand. Their behavior is like a mirror that, without ever lying, reflects their inner worlds.

Is not communism, a system built upon the skulls of twenty-million victims, a reflection of a brutal heart? Are not the pyramids, graveyards for thousands just for the sake of one pharaoh, in fact atrocious monuments of oppression? For the many unmindful, they still amount to historical masterpieces that leave reason in awe. But considered from the vantage of the truth, do not they betray a portrait of cruelty, vicious enough to shock and frighten the most savage hyenas?

Proved by all this is the fact that once frogs rein supreme in society, everywhere turns into a swamp. When snake and scorpion like temperaments hold sway, society is exposed to their venom, instigating terror and anarchy. But if rose like temperaments govern proceedings, then the whole land turns into garden, reconciling society with peace.

The training of Revelation is therefore imperative. Those remote from such training, even if they do not exhibit displays of brutality and instead show signs of certain right conduct, always carry the potential of brutal behavior; for except for Divine training, all goodness acquired passes by. In times of difficulty, when egoistic desires run ravage, the crudeness and potential for the bad in those devoid of that sublime training transpire, to the light of day. An untrained ego resembles a cat with an appetite for a mouse; a cat that does not think twice about abandoning the exquisite food put in front of him, just upon the sight of a mouse, leaping ahead to pursue it, without hesitation. A human being is no different; lacking the training of divine measure, regardless of the numerous beauties the heart may be fond of, once the cat like ego is enticed by a mouse, however distant, it bids the heart to pursue it, at the cost of devastation. The lives of Pharaoh and Nimrod are but displays of coldhearted massacres, motivated by desires the size of mice.

A far cry that is from Divine training, which, let alone condoning the killing of innocent humans, commands delicacy, like a shivering candle, even against a slight infringement of the rights of others. The Blessed Messenger ﷺ refrained from even severing a green branch. On the way to the conquest of Mecca, he commanded his army to proceed from the other side of the road, in order not to frighten a dog suckling her pups. Distraught by the sight of an ants nest burnt to ashes, it was again the Noble Prophet ﷺ to remark, "*Who could do such a horrible thing?*" Immersed in the spirit of the Prophet

ﷺ, sculpted by his clay of compassion, the Ottomans founded numerous *waqfs*, self-funded charity foundations epitomizing the zenith of mercy in their service, both for humans and animals alike. There were even *waqfs* established just for the purpose of caring for and nurturing animals. It is of little wonder today that we see reports, made by travelers journeying through the Ottoman dominions at the time, attesting to how cats and dogs were always lingering around people in Muslim neighborhoods, while in other quarters, they would look for places to hide at the sight of the shadow of a human being.

These are all manifestations of the level of matured training one has, or lack of it. Shedding enough blood to water the ground with it, is man; yet it is also man who gives his own blood to the save the life of the needy.

Though containing an intrinsic wisdom, in life, people of positive and negative characters endure together. To use an example, this resembles the agony forced upon a fawn locked in a barn full of brutish, grumbling beasts. Sometimes a generous coexists with a miser; at times it is a wise with a fool, or even a benevolent with an oppressor. The miser has little compassion; a coward, he lacks commitment. A generous, alternatively, is compassionate, humble and committed. The fool does not understand the wise. The oppressor thinks he acts with justice, a ready excuse to use force to crush those around him. In short, the angelic spirited survive together, in this worldly life, with hyenas; the former proceeding on the path of making acquaintance with and becoming a servant of the Real, the latter lost in the deception of assuming a life dominated by the habit of low creatures to be happiness, in a life controlled by consumption, lust and greed of the like.

Living in a world inhabited by opposite characters, in essence, is a difficult test; a test, however, a person is compelled to overcome. Passing the test of the world and being reunited with the Divine is the essential purpose human existence, which in turn requires one to slip away from bad attributes and obtain those that are praised, and thus live with the honor and dignity worthy of a human being.

Although spirit wise celestial, the body of a human being is of earth. Thus once the spirit returns to Allah, glory unto Him, so shall the body return into earth. Bodily, man carries the features of other organisms, the precise reason why the ego must be curbed through a spiritual training and refining and thereby feed and hence strengthen the spirit. Otherwise, one cannot be immune to becoming a victim, externally of Satan and internally of the transgressions of the ego, which then puts the spirit in a weak position.

The Quran states:

"And the soul and Him Who made it perfect…Then He inspired it to understand what is right and wrong for it; he will indeed be successful who purifies it, and he will indeed fail who corrupts it." (as-Shams, 7-10)

The great Mawlana Rumi explains the right and the wrong residing in the inner world made mention by the *ayah* through the following analogy:

"If you want the truth, o striver on the path of the Real, then know that neither Musa nor the Pharaoh are dead; they are well alive within you, concealed in your existence, continuing their battle in your heart. You therefore must search for these rivals within yourself!"

He goes on:

"Do not look to feed the flesh, in excess, and develop it...for it is a sacrifice destined for earth. Seek instead to nourish your heart, for it is that which is destined for high above, with honor.

Give little of what is sweet and fatty to the flesh. For those who feed it in excess are ultimate preys to the desires of the ego, and are lost into shame.

Feed the spirit with spiritual nourishment. Offer it mature thought, delicate understanding and like food, so that it leaves to its destination with strength."

An untrained ego is like a tree with rotten roots, signs of which are visible in its branches, leaves and fruits. A disease in the heart comes to light through the deeds of the body, spreading its harm. Symptoms of it are malice, jealousy, conceit and other attributes of the ego, awaiting necessary treatment. Rectifying these deficiencies become possible, firstly, through entering the path willed and shown by Allah, glory unto Him.

The two most basic tendencies allowing a human being to construct her character compliant with the pleasure of the Almighty are taking example and imitation.

The Tendencies of Taking Example and Imitation

From the moment he is born, man stands in need of an example. All ideas, beliefs and activities that shape a person's life like language, religion, moral behavior and habits are developed through none other than surrounding examples and impressions received therefrom. Minor exceptions aside, this is generally the case. A child, for instance, only learns the language spoken by her parents; learning a second, a third or even a fourth language thereafter requires other examples. So in a sense, among other lesser factors, the education of a person consists in none other than getting her, as much as is allowed by the innate tendency of imitation, to imitate what is on offer to be taught, be it good or bad. This way, depending on her capacity to come under the influence of and imitate parents, relatives and the social environment, a person becomes either a good or a bad member of society.

Yet while there is relative ease in learning a language and other external skills, serious barriers impede the shaping of one's religious, moral and spiritual world. Therefore, as long as this realm is not allowed to be trained by prophets and friends of the Real, a human being cannot resist being dragged into the ditch of ignorance and rebellion, turning their potential for eternal bliss to a miserable disaster.

The condition of those who take certain celebrities, swimming in the swamp of overindulgence, as role models and try to become like them, much to the peril of both themselves and their eternity, suggests a reckless waste of human potential and corruption of civilization. This is but a laying waste to the heart by instating on its throne, left empty and abandoned, the wrong people just for the sake of occupying it with something.

Enveloping the tricks of the ego in concrete examples, Mawlana Rumi –quddisa sirruh- illustrates below the strangeness in which man is deceived:

"*It is of no surprise that a lamb flees from a wolf, for the wolf is its enemy and hunter. But for lamb to fall in love with a wolf... that merits wonder.*"

"Many a fish, while assuredly swimming in water, is caught by a hook, victim to the greed of its appetite."

Humankind is therefore always in need of guides, with an elegance of heart and a refined spirit, to teach them of the tricks of the ego.

The Exemplary Characters of Prophets

As feeling affection for a person, admiring and trying to imitate his character is a tendency that arises from natural disposition, it is crucial for human beings to find the most perfect examples and follow their lead. It is for such reason that Allah, glory unto Him, the eternally Munificent, has not only blessed mankind with books of Revelation, but He has also sent prophets, living embodiments of those books, endowed with innumerable and supreme attributes.

They are such consummate personalities that they exude a perfection of behavior, in religion, knowledge and morality. Throughout history, each of these prophets has rendered exceptional service to humankind by virtue of excelling in certain exemplary conduct.

As for saints, the heirs of prophets and friends of the Real, they are wise, righteous and mature Believers who have:

Impeccably fused the esoteric and the exoteric of Religion which they have embroidered onto their personalities;

Reached a perfection of conduct through covering great distances with their hearts on the road of abstinence and piety;

Attained a depth of feeling and the zest of faith by virtue of extending their cognition and comprehension to the horizons of both worlds;

And whose entire resolve is to save humankind from bad conduct and the dark gutter of the ego and elevate them to good morals, the skies of spiritual maturity. They are the peaks of the behavioral perfection, taught by prophets spread across times, towering personalities to be taken after, for those who have not been fortunate to see a prophet. The teachings and advice they articulate in the language of mercy that revitalize hearts are essentially drops of spirituality, dripping forth from the font of prophethood.

Whenever one sees justice prevailing in a given society, whichever it may be throughout the world, a bond of mercy and compassion binding hearts together, or in a given society, if the rich run to the aid of the poor, the strong protect the weak, the healthy lend a helping hand to the ill and, again, the well-to-do feed the orphans, without a shadow of a doubt, these virtues have been handed own by prophets and those walking on their path.

The family of mankind that begun with Adam and Hawwa –alayhimassalam-, adopted as the foremost place of worship the area on which today stands the Holy Kabah, in Mecca. Spread across the world thereafter out of natural and social needs, guided from time to time by prophets, the Children of Adam continued their life of religion. As often as Divine Truths were tampered with by the ignorant, the Almighty sent prophets, through whom He effaced the tampering and revived religion. Continually saved throughout history from individual and social disarray, a mark of Divine Grace, humanity thus reached the Final Epoch.

Making its entrance into the world at long awaited last, at *asr* mark of its entire history, was then the *Asr'us-Saadah*, the Age of Bliss, presenting, at the very place where religious life had once inaugurated, a final display, the zenith of perfection this time, with the Blessed Muhammad Mustafa ﷺ. Inconceivable, it would be, to imagine a perfection beyond that of his, insofar as with him, the regular revival of religion through the sending of prophets came to an end, making Islam the religion Allah, glory unto Him, is pleased with.

We can therefore say that the Noble Messenger ﷺ, having embodied and actualized innumerable instances of virtue in his life, stands as the most perfect example to cater for the natural tendency of imitation within human beings. Success in imitating him is undoubtedly dependent upon an infatuation with his character and a wholehearted love.

How Much Do We Love Him?

Using the Heart and the Reason

The Almighty has rendered human beings unique, granting them the rank of *ahsan'ul-taqwim*, the cream of creation, in whose service, as He has moreover declared, are whatever there is on earth and in the skies. But of course, these are for those who can think.

What this means is that our greatest duty lies in contemplating the blessings given us by Allah, glory unto Him, and evaluating them in accordance with the purpose for which they have been given. In particular, we are obliged to put our heart and reason to the most proper use.

What is the proper use of reason?

Reason must not be slave to the ego; rather, through an acquaintance with divine realities, it should rise to the awareness of being in a world of trial.

What is the proper use of heart?

The heart is the precinct of Real Love, the point of view of the Divine. It therefore must be kept free of all else, pure from sin and filled with *dhikr* and *tawhid*, thus be returned to Divine presence in its purity. And for such a blend:

The Sole Example...The Blessed Prophet ﷺ

For the purpose of warning and imparting awareness, the Almighty has sent prophets, around a 124,000 in number up until fifteen centuries ago, an indication of His Boundless Generosity. The prophet He most loved, the most impeccable and the most unique, He left till last. Each prophet was sent to certain people, guiding them in accordance with their social structure. The Messenger of Allah ﷺ, on the other hand, has been sent to entire humankind, with the time until the end of human history entrusted in his guiding light.

At a time when disbelief and ignorance was at the depths of despair, Allah sent him as a one man guide for mankind, just like the sun, presenting him as the most splendid gift.

The Greatest of All Miracles

Allah, glory unto Him, granted the Prophet with the greatest miracle of all: The Holy Quran. The Quran itself will prove being Word of Allah and the truth of His Messenger's prophethood till the Day of Resurrection; until when all human beings shall witness the miracle and gain an insight to it.

The Prophet constructed such a society with the miracle of the Quran that it has come to be known as the society of the Age of Bliss. No similar case in history exists. From the dregs of an ignorant people, there was produced a virtuous society of previously unimaginable magnitude, much like a rise from the base of the Indian Ocean to the summit of the Himalayas. The spiritually inspiring education of the Prophet ﷺ imparted such sensitivity of feeling, compassion and responsibility that a wild mob who previously buried their own daughters alive could no longer bear even the mauling of a weak lamb by a wolf at the shore of Tigris. Simply this example could suffice as testimony to the greatness of the Blessed Prophet's ﷺ character and how quintessential of an example he has set.

The Blind Vilify the Sun

Hearts will certainly see the Blessed Prophet ﷺ, given they are not blind. Unless they are cross eyed, they will not be able to find in him the least deficiency. Those who try to point the finger at him only point the finger at their own faults and deficiencies.

History abounds in disgusting slanders made against prophets by their own people. As the Divine Truths they communicated did not comply with the egoistic desires of certain people, they were discomforted by the beauty of revelation. They were thus in an attempt to malign prophets with their own shortcomings and ugliness, in order to ensure that the egocentric lives they lead gained legitimate acceptance.

Thus likewise, the entirety of the ugly campaigns of slander launched against the Blessed Prophet ﷺ today, reflect nothing other than the contemptibility and misery of the slanderers themselves.

Beings can only survive in a habitat suitable for their nature; and human beings are no exception. Just as it is unfeasible to get a honeybee to live anywhere other than its world of pollens and flowers where it both feeds and breathes, it is inconceivable to expect a rat, whose nature is fit only for filth, to dwell in a rose garden. Grand spirits are nourished through the inspiration that springs from the Muhammadan Truth, while wicked souls are content with dirt.

At times, Abu Bakr ﷺ would look at Noble Prophet's ﷺ face, filled with admiration, and remark 'how beautiful!'. In essence, through that mirror he was only gazing at his inner world. Indeed, his emotional reply to the Prophet of Mercy ﷺ when he said, "*I have not advantaged from the possessions of anyone else than that of Abu Bakr*", showed that he had in fact devoted all his existence to the Prophet of Allah ﷺ and had become annihilated in him:

"*Are not I and my possessions for your sake alone, Messenger of Allah?*" (Ibn Majah, Muqaddimah, 11) His inner world was but a mirror reflection the morality of the Gracious Prophet ﷺ.

Abu Jahl, on the other hand, the archenemy of Allah and His Messenger, would receive a totally opposite impression from that wonderful face, oblivious to its beauty and splendor. The difference there is that it was their own realities, that is to say their inner worlds, both saw in the Mirror of Muhammad ﷺ; for prophets are like shiny mirrors, through which each person gazes at his inner world. Mirrors do not lie for anyone; neither do they display the ugly as beautiful, nor the beautiful as ugly. They only reveal whatever is mirrored onto it.

Confronted by the power and majesty of Allah, glory unto Him, who has taken Islam under the might of His protection, it is certain that those attempting to defy the Blessed Prophet, the Quran, and Muslims alike, are sooner or later doomed to be struck with Divine vengeance.

Obvious is the enormous degree of insult caused upon innocent Muslim hearts brimming over with love for the

Noble Prophet ﷺ by tongues of venom and pens of senselessness, which from time to time spit out the poison of their sinister inner worlds.

It should also be well known that it is impossible to destroy the inclination towards truth granted to human nature by the Almighty. However much irreligiousness may be advanced through coercion, it cannot be successful in preventing the flourishing of religious feeling, rooted deep within the spirit and conscience. The need for the servant to gain closeness to the Creator shatters all restriction, a sublime natural sentiment that recognizes no bounds; simply for the reason that Divine Power has willed the need for religion and seeking nearness to the Lord as part of *sunnatullah*, the unchanging law of the Almighty.

Mawlana Rumi vividly depicts the heedless, who turn a blind eye to the Real and pointlessly try to snuff out divine light:

"To vilify the sun that brightens up our world, to search for its defect is but to vilify oneself, to admit to being blind, having both eyes that see only darkness."

"When Allah wills to tear someone to shreds, to expose their shame, He throws in his heart the want to condemn people of purity."

Let alone abstaining from vilifying the Noble Prophet ﷺ, humankind should be instead thinking of ways to express its gratitude for him. Truly, a heart is not a heart that is not filled with feelings of appreciation seeing him shiver for the salvation of humanity, from his birth to his very final breath.

The compassion the Prophet of Mercy ﷺ nurtured for us was certainly far greater than that of parents for their children. The Prophet ﷺ who says no other human being has been threatened and subjected to a greater agony and hunger more than him (Tirmidhi, Qiyamat, 34/2472); his conscience nonetheless bears no personal complaints, apart from a heart burning on behalf of his suffering *ummah*. Such a compassionate and thoughtful prophet he is that, like he has striven in this world for the sake of us receiving forgiveness and salvation, so shall he fall prostrate before the Throne on the Day of Resurrection, tearfully pleading Allah, glory unto Him, until his wish of interceding for his *ummah* is granted.[56]

In gratitude for a prophet who makes a supreme effort to intercede on behalf of our forgiveness, both in Here and the Hereafter, should not we also make a supreme effort to become Believers of the kind he envisaged, hold him more precious than even ourselves and become infatuated with his love?

A Lover Follows the Beloved

"*One is with whom he loves*" states a hadith. (Bukhari, Adab, 96) Now how much do we love our Blessed Prophet ﷺ?

Of course, this kind of love should be understood as togetherness shared between the lover and beloved. Togetherness, in the truest sense of the word, requires a mutual resemblance through a transmission of *hal*, a commonness of character. One is together with whom he loves in essence, in every word spoken, as well as behavior, in feelings and thought and no less in living itself.

56. See, Bukhârî, Anbiyâ, 3, 9; Mislim, Îmân, 327, 328; Tirmidhî, Qiyâmat, 10.

Lacking this kind of togetherness where the lover assumes a different path to that of the beloved, then the lover is not really with the beloved, for he feels no love, in the truest sense.

Accordingly then how much do we love our One and Only Prophet ﷺ? How much do we embrace his Sunnah? To what extent do we explain him to our children and our surroundings? What degree of a togetherness of heart do we have with two of his greatest legacies, the Quran and the *Ahl'ul-Bayt*? How much of a resemblance do our homes have to the homes of *Ahl'ul-Bayt*, permeated with the spirituality of Sunnah?

Following Him Requires an Education of the Heart

To attain bliss both in this turbulent world and in the field of resurrection, the turf of fright, we stand under an imperative need to take after the Noble Prophet ﷺ in all aspects of our lives, be it social, domestic or work related. He is the sole example for human beings, from the lowest to the highest ends the social scale. How are we to be like him? Simply through reading from paper? No. Rather immersing our hearts in his education; an education whose method the Almighty clearly reveals in the Quran:

"Certainly you have in the Messenger of Allah a quintessential example for him who hopes in Allah and the Latter Day and remembers Allah much." (Ahzab, 21)

So the first requirement is to hope in Allah, glory unto Him; in reuniting with Him. The remembrance of giving an account for our deeds in Divine Presence should always accompany our conscience.

The second requirement is to hope in the Latter Day, the Hereafter, with a certain belief. We must grasp mortality and overcome its bounds, expressed beautifully by Mawlana Rumi:

"The life of the world is but a dream. Becoming wealthy there is like chancing upon treasure in a dream. Possessions, passed on from one generation to another, eventually stay put in the world."

It is therefore vital that we are aware of existence in a world of trial and through setting aside the desires of the ego thereby, turn out hearts into voyagers of eternity. We must acquire such a blend that the Hereafter, for us, should become a field of reunion. And for such education, it is necessary we obtain a share of the *uswat'ul-hasanah*, the quintessential example of the Noble Prophet ﷺ. Only then does the Almighty promise us His Paradise and bless us with reunion with His Beauty.

As for the third requirement, it is a constant remembrance of Allah, glory unto Him. The heart needs to continually be with the Almighty. How often? The answer to that is hinted in a verse as being as often as, "when they stand, and when they sit, and when they lie down to sleep" (Ali Imran, 191) In other words, constantly; a unceasing consciousness of being under Divine surveillance. True, our Lord is closer to us than our jugular vein, though how close are we to Him? It is in instituting precisely that closeness that we need to take the example of the Blessed Prophet ﷺ.

The Prophet of Allah's ﷺ Value and Us

There is no way of covering distance towards Allah without comprehending and being trained in the value and honor of the Blessed Messenger ﷺ. Allah, glory unto Him, places especial accent on the value with which He Himself sees the Prophet ﷺ:

"Allah and His angels send blessings on the Prophet: O Believers! Send your blessings on him and salute him with all respect." (al-Ahzab, 56)

The Almighty, too, sends His blessings to the Blessed Prophet ﷺ, to the noblest of all His creation, with the angels joining in. Comprehending the true nature of what that might be is impossible for our hearts, consciences and understanding alike. How does Allah, glory unto Him, send His blessings to a being He created? Together with some explanation afforded regarding the matter, in truth, it is a Divine Enigma. But one thing is for certain that the Almighty nurtures an exceptional love and care for the Blessed Messenger ﷺ, something He wants us to be aware of as well, commanding:

"O Believers! Send your blessings on him and salute him with all respect."

But these blessings and salutes ought not to be made merely with the tongue. Rather, one's entire existence should be a virtual blessing on and a salutation of him. Our behavior in all social dealings, whether it is at home or work, should transpire in a way worthy of being a blessing and a salutation for the Prophet of Grace ﷺ.

One should stop to self-critically think, for instance, to what degree would the Noble Prophet ﷺ consent to one's dealings with family, in business and treatment of other human beings in general? Or to the manner in which one raises her children? Or to the quality of one's deeds of worship?

If we fail to interrogate ourselves and our hearts and weigh them up against questions today, sure to be much more terrifying is the weighing up and the interrogation of the Day of Resurrection; a day in which it will be declared:

اِقْرَاْ كِتَابَكَ كَفٰى بِنَفْسِكَ الْيَوْمَ عَلَيْكَ حَسِيبًا

"Read your book; your own self is sufficient as a reckoner against you this day" (al-Isra, 14)

Our book of deeds will expose who we really are, in all its frankness, with not a secret left unexposed. We will watch the film that has been our lives, viewing the performance of our salats, our fasts, and so forth, in all their barren actualities. We shall see, then, whether we simply paid lip service to servanthood or were indeed triumphant in putting our heart and soul into performing our primary duty. We will see what we did, during life, in appreciation of the innumerable blessings of the Almighty upon us, observing just how much of the spirit, reason, wit and wealth we were able to let others in on and how much of it we put to waste. We will know first hand how much we were able to love Allah and His Messenger and equal to the task of being enshrouded in their character.

All this will be shown us in the very near future in our book of deeds, screened on the monitors of the Hereafter. And then:

"Till, when they reach it, their ears and their eyes and their skins testify against them as to what they used to do." (Fussilat, 20)

We must therefore constantly cross-examine ourselves.

What do our eyes watch?

How much of Divine Revelation and Prophetic Advice do our ears listen to?

To what extent are we using our bodies and opportunities in the way of the Real?

More important is to assess ourselves and take necessary precaution while there is still opportunity at hand.

The Trial of Love and *Adab*

Human beings are in a world of trial. To be sure, the world is but a school of Divine test, an important phase of which comprises loving, obeying and upholding proper manners, or *adab*, towards the Blessed Prophet ﷺ. Thus declares the Almighty:

"O Believers! Obey Allah and obey the messenger, and render not your actions vain." (Muhammad, 33)

"O Believers! Do not raise your voices above the voice of the Prophet, and do not speak loud to him as you speak loud to one another, lest your deeds became null while you do not perceive. Surely those who lower their voices before Allah's Messenger, are they whose hearts Allah has proved for guarding (against evil); they shall have forgiveness and a great reward. As for those who call out to you from behind the private chambers, surely most of them do not understand." (al-Hujurat, 2-4)

It turns out that our courtesy for the Noble Messenger of Allah ﷺ, strive to know him more personally and adherence to his Sunnah is a test of piety for our hearts, and no less, a means for nearness to Allah, glory unto Him...

It turns also out that only the mindless, dimwitted can dare to be rude to the Blessed Prophet ﷺ and yell at him from a distance.

Another outcome we can draw from there is with regard to how we should take the Messenger of Allah ﷺ as example, and the manner in which we should weigh up our lives against his. The clear command of the Quran in relation is:

"Whoever obeys the Messenger, he indeed obeys Allah, and whoever turns back, so We have not sent you as a keeper over them." (an-Nisa, 80)

The Measure of Loving Him

The incident recounted by Abdullah ibn Hisham ؓ is significant for indicating the intensity with which one ought to love the Noble Messenger ﷺ:

"We were once with the Messenger of Allah ﷺ. He was sitting, holding Omar's ؓ hand in his own. Then Omar ؓ suddenly remarked:

'You are dearer to me than everything, Messenger of Allah, except for myself', to express his love.

'*No*', responded the Messenger of Allah ﷺ. '*By Allah, under whose Power and Will I abide, you will not have truly believed until I become dearer to you than your own self.*'

'Then, by Allah', Omar ؓ immediately said, 'you are now dearer to me than myself'. The Messenger of Allah ﷺ thereupon assured:

'*Now it is, Omar, as it should be!*'" (Bukhari, Ayman, 3)

That is the measure of love and affection with which we ought to follow the Blessed Prophet ﷺ, crowning him on the throne of our hearts, letting him be the guide of our lives. Loving him has been decreed compulsory.[57] The Quran states:

اَلنَّبِيُّ اَوْلٰى بِالْمُؤْمِنِينَ مِنْ اَنْفُسِهِمْ

"The Prophet is closer to the Believers than their own selves…" (al-Ahzab, 6)

He is closer and dearer to us than our own selves.

Loving the Blessed Prophet ﷺ has therefore also been cited as a condition of true belief.

"*By Allah, under whose Power and Will I abide, one will not have truly believed until I become dearer to him than his mother, father, children and everybody else.*" (Bukhari, Iman, 8)

The Companions would thus race to fulfill even the smallest desire of the Messenger of Allah ﷺ, justifying their love at every given opportunity, with each exclaiming, "May my mother, father, my life and whatever I have, Messenger of Allah, be sacrificed in your way!"

To remain indifferent to this love or worse still, to react rudely to it, is a mark of ignorance. Clutching onto it, on the other hand, will prove an eternal cure.

57. See, at-Tawba, 24.

The Mark of Loving Him

One continuously talks about what or whoever it is that he loves, exploiting every opportunity to describe it to those around.

A businessman caught up in work always speaks about his trades and dealings, how much he supposedly earned or lost; where there is money to be made or wasted, and so forth. Some adore their children, talking about them wherever and whenever.

But the distinguished Companions and the righteous, with great admiration, always talked about the Blessed Prophet ﷺ, with whom they were infatuated, taking an inexplicable enjoyment out of it.

There, is a love of the Prophet ﷺ, permeated with an enthusiasm to know and imitate him and to be with him in the Hereafter. May Allah bless us also with an enthusiasm to know and love him…Amin…

Another secret of 'love', the reason of the existence of being, lies in the lover adopting the *hal*, the inner state, of the loved. Whatever lack of capability and power a lover may be withheld by, she will attain a result in accordance with the caliber of the one loved.

The Difficulty of Properly Explaining Him

Commanding a small force, Khalid ibn Walid ؓ had once stopped over next to a Muslim clan. The chief of the clan asked him to explain the Blessed Prophet ﷺ.

"It lies beyond my power to explain the beauties of the Messenger of Allah", replied Khalid ؓ. "If you are expecting a proper explanation that is impossible."

"Explain as much as you can. Make it short and to the point then", said the chief, prompting Khalid ؓ to give the following reply:

اَلرَّسُولُ عَلٰى قَدْرِ الْمُرْسِلِ

"The Sent is appropriate with the honor of the Sender..." (Since the sender is the Lord of the Worlds, the Creator of the Universe, then you imagine the honor of the sent!)[58]

May Allah grant our hearts shares of the love of the Companions for the Blessed Prophet ﷺ! Through the love of our Prophet ﷺ, may He cast beauty upon our lives!

Amin...

58. Munâwî, V, 92/6478; Kastalânî, *Mevâhib-i Ledünniyye Tercümesi*, İstanbul 1984, p. 417.

Conclusion

To be worthy recipients of the grand intercession of the Blessed Messenger of Allah ﷺ, we need to reconsider where we stand with respect to adhering to him, and weighing up our lives against the standards aforementioned set by the Prophet ﷺ, adopt a profound contemplation and perseverance. Abounding with an enthusiasm to lead a life that befits his *ummah*, we need to try and reflect his unique magnificence onto our deeds of worship, behavior, feelings and thoughts; to our present and future, to our world as well as the Hereafter. One only imitates the loved one to the degree of his infatuation. In order to properly follow and imitate the Light of Being ﷺ, it is therefore vital we become acquainted with him in a real sense and try to assess his exemplary character.

However much a land may be fit for agriculture, it will not offer harvest without there passing over it rain clouds, the sun and the accompanying fresh breeze of spring. Like a fertile strip of land, for the heart to become productive, it must receive the downpour of the one, sent as a quintessential example for humankind.

The Blessed Prophet ﷺ is the most supreme of all those before him, and those to come after. The inexhaustible source of virtue, he is the reason of all blessings and mercies granted upon Earth. It was to him that the Holy Quran, replete with the eternal truths, was revealed, and passed therefrom to the realm of Belief.

The final conclusion to be drawn from all this is that no amount of respect shown to the Blessed Messenger ﷺ, even to things that simply remind us a little of him, is enough. After all, the Great Prophet ﷺ has been granted the accolade of being the beloved of Allah, the Transcendent, surpassing all imagination and cognition. Thus even coming close to the value and perfection of that grand Prophet, to whom the Creator of the universe, in tandem with His innumerable angels, sends his blessings and salute, to fit him into comprehension with the limited possibilities offered by words, is inconceivable.

In truth, there is no other way than to humbly resign, from explaining his sublime nature, to an eternal silence. While languages confess their inadequacy in his depiction, the words spilling from our tongue could only be, at best, an expression of a drop, from a vast ocean, that has trickled forth into our understanding.

Joy to those Believers who do not give their hearts away to anyone other than the Messenger of Allah ﷺ, and are not deceived by the phony flowers of fake gardens…

Let's turn to our Lord by breathing his spirituality at every breath…

Let's plead to our Lord with the love of the Prophet ﷺ as testimony…

Blessings to Muhammad Mustafa, the Master of Both Worlds…

Blessings to Muhammad Mustafa, the Prophet of Man and Jinn…

Blessings to Muhammad Mustafa, the Leader of the Sacred Lands...

Blessings to Muhammad Mustafa, the grandfather of Hasan and Huseyn...

اَللّٰهُمَّ صَلِّ عَلٰى مُحَمَّدٍ وَعَلٰى اٰلِهٖ
وَصَحْبِهٖ وَبَارِكْ وَسَلِّمْ

May Allah, glory unto Him, allow us to receive a proper share of the exemplary character of His Blessed Prophet ﷺ, our eternal guide of bliss, and to crown our Here and Hereafter with reflections of his beautiful conduct! May He let drops of inspiration trickle forth into our hearts from his profound spirituality! May our hearts be eternal grounds for the love of Allah and His Messenger! May Allah bless us all with His Messenger's ﷺ grand intercession!

Amin...

Contents

Foreword 7

Part One / 13

The Exemplar beyond Compare 15

Prophet Muhammad Mustafa ﷺ
Uswat'ul-Hasanah / The Quintessential Example 25

Part Two / 39

The Towering Morals of the Prophet of Allah ﷺ 41

The Prophet of Allah's ﷺ
Beauty of Countenance and Morals 42

The Humbleness of the Prophet of Allah ﷺ 48

The Generosity of the Prophet of Allah ﷺ 51

The Piety of the Prophet of Allah ﷺ 53

The Prophet of Allah's ﷺ Life of Abstinence 55

The Courtesy of the Prophet of Allah ﷺ 58

The Manners and Haya of the Prophet of Allah ﷺ 62

The Courage of the Prophet of Allah ﷺ 64

The Gentleness of the Prophet of Allah ﷺ 66

The Mercy and Compassion of the
Prophet of Allah ﷺ 68

The Lenience of the Prophet of Allah ﷺ 70
The Prophet of Allah's ﷺ Observance of Neighbor's Rights 74
The Prophet of Allah's ﷺ Treatment of the Poor 75
The Prophet of Allah's ﷺ Treatment of Captives and Servants 78
The Prophet of Allah's ﷺ Treatment of Women 83
The Prophet of Allah's ﷺ Treatment of Orphans 88
The Prophet of Allah's ﷺ Treatment of Animals 89
Standards from the Stars 96

Part Three / 99

The Heart's Blend in Following the Prophet of Allah ﷺ 101
Adhering to the Prophet of Allah ﷺ with Love 104
The Mirror of His Love and Morals: Asr'us-Saadah 109
Touching Hymns of Prophetic Love 116
The Companions' Love of the Prophet of Allah ﷺ 120
The Fountain of Love after the Companions 133
Salawat'us-Sharifah 144

Part Four / 149

The Greatest Need for the Heart and the Mind: An Exemplary Character 151
The Education that Makes Man: Divine Teaching 151
The Tendencies of Taking Example and Imitation 159
The Exemplary Characters of Prophets 161
How Much Do We Love Him? 164

Using the Heart and the Reason 164
The Sole Example...The Blessed Prophet ﷺ 165
The Greatest of All Miracles 165
The Blind Vilify the Sun 166
A Lover Follows the Beloved 169
Following Him Requires an Education of the Heart 170
The Prophet of Allah's ﷺ Value and Us 171
The Trial of Love and Adab 174
The Measure of Loving Him 175
The Mark of Loving Him 177
The Difficulty of Properly Explaining Him 177
Conclusion 179